For Christ's Crown

FOR
CHRIST'S
CROWN

*Sketches of Puritans
and Covenanters*

RICHARD M. HANNULA

canonpress
Moscow, Idaho

Published by Canon Press
P.O. Box 8729, Moscow, ID 83843
800.488.2034 | www.canonpress.com

Richard M. Hannula, *For Christ's Crown: Sketches of Puritans and Covenanters*
Copyright © 2014 by Richard M. Hannula.

Cover and interior design by James Engerbretson.
Cover painting "Donald Cargill" by Forrest Dickison.
Interior illustrations by Forrest Dickison.

Printed in the United States of America.

Library of Congress Cataloging-in-Publication Data is forthcoming.

14 15 16 17 18 19 20   9 8 7 6 5 4 3 2 1

With love to my grandchildren:
Nathan, Anna, and Josiah, and to those
who will follow in their train.

CONTENTS

INTRODUCTION

Why should 21st century Christians be interested in English and Scottish believers who lived 400 years ago? Because the Puritans and Covenanters left an impressive legacy of gospel preaching, heavenly-mindedness, and holiness. They set a standard for devotion to Jesus Christ and biblical understanding that has been largely unmatched since.

The Puritans and the Covenanters believed that the Bible alone was the Christian's guide for knowing the will of God, and that Scripture truth was there to be understood and applied by all. One Puritan pastor told his flock, "Think in every line you read that God is speaking to you." Not content to scratch the surface of any particular teaching of the Bible, they labored to get to the bottom. The thoroughness and precision in which they articulated biblical doctrines in their preaching and writing are unparalleled in church history.

Three primary biblical doctrines laid the foundation for their understanding of life:

1. All people are mired in sin, deserve the wrath of God, and are without hope apart from the mercy of God.

2. Forgiveness through the redeeming love of Christ is solely a gift of God's grace.

3. Gratitude for salvation must press the Christian on to holiness.

A profound awareness of their own sin gave rise to a deep love for Christ and his sacrificial death to pay the penalty for sin. Puritans and Covenanters centered their preaching and teaching on the cross. An early Puritan, Richard Greenham, said that the goal of preaching was to "drive men out of themselves and send them to Christ." Trusting that God by his grace saves sinners, they preached the good news of Jesus Christ with clarity and boldness. They knew that Christ would save everyone that his heavenly Father had given him and that no one could snatch them out of his hand.

These pastors worked not only to save souls, but also to bring believers to Christian maturity. Knowing that Christ called them to obey His commandments, they made repentance and holiness their chief aims. Shunning idleness, they strove to redeem the time that God had given them, making the most of each day as those who must give an account to God. Their disciplined lives of morning and evening devotions of praise, prayer, and Bible study established a model that present-day Christians would be wise to follow.

English Puritans and Scottish Covenanters endeavored to purify and protect their churches from the controlling influence of the Crown. The Stuart monarchs tried, with increasing pressure, to force high church worship and hierarchy onto all their subjects. The Puritans and the Covenanters struggled in the face of persecution to honor Christ and promote biblical Christianity. In Scotland, thousands were put to death. In England, many suffered imprisonment and loss of property. Most stayed in their homeland and endured the trials that fell upon them. Some fled to Europe or crossed the Atlantic to begin anew in the wilderness of North America.

Through it all, they cultivated an eternal perspective, setting their minds on things above, where Christ is seated at the right hand of the Father. They taught that believers here on earth are strangers and aliens on a pilgrimage to heaven. The Puritan Richard Baxter advised his flock to meditate on Christ reigning in heaven, saying that it "deserved a thousand thousand thoughts."

The following biographical sketches show Puritan and Covenanter beliefs and traits in flesh and blood. The author hopes that readers, both young and old, will be inspired to learn more about these stalwart Christians and seek to follow in their steps as they followed in Christ's. George Whitefield, the great eighteenth century evangelist, called the Puritans "burning and shining lights." They were indeed.

OVERVIEW

THE DEFENDERS OF BIBLICAL WORSHIP:

PURITANS: English Protestants in the 16th and 17th centuries who believed that the English Reformation had not gone far enough to purify the Church of England from its unbiblical practices and doctrines left over from Roman Catholicism. The Puritans believed that Christ alone was the head of the church, and He alone ordained how He was to be worshiped. The Puritans resisted the intrusion of any belief or worship feature into the life of the church that could not be found in the Scriptures.

COVENANTERS: Scottish Presbyterians of the 17th century who opposed the efforts of the Stuart kings to force practices of worship and church government upon the Church of Scotland which they believed to be contrary to the teachings of the Bible. Although the Covenanters did not always agree upon the best way to promote their goals, they all supported the National Covenant (1638) in which they pledged to resist the king's efforts to introduce anything into the Scottish church "to the ruin of the true reformed religion and of our liberties, laws and estates." The motto and rallying cry of the Covenanters was "For Christ's Crown and Covenant."

THE MONARCHS:

ELIZABETH I (Queen of England, 1558-1603)—The Reformation in England (1520s-1550s) separated the Church of England from the Roman Catholic Church. Protestant reformers pressed Henry VIII and Edward VI to reform the church according to the Scriptures. When Edward died in 1553, his half-sister Mary took the throne. She tried to force the Church of England back into the fold of the Roman Catholic Church. Her government executed hundreds of Protestants and thousands more fled the country. When Mary died in 1558, Elizabeth became queen. Elizabeth restored the Protestant faith, but she insisted in following a middle way between Catholic rituals and practices and the faith and worship called for by the Protestant reformers. The Act of Supremacy of 1559 declared Elizabeth "Supreme Governor of the Church of England," and the Act of Uniformity forced all citizens to follow the worship ceremonies laid down by church officials in the Book of Common Prayer.

Ministers and parishioners who pressed Elizabeth and her church leaders to purify the church of unbiblical practices became known as Puritans. Elizabeth fiercely resisted the Puritans' reform efforts, and ejected hundreds of Puritan ministers from their churches.

JAMES VI (King of Scotland, 1567-1625) had been King of Scotland for twenty-five years when Queen Elizabeth of England died childless. James was the nearest heir to the throne and in 1603, he was crowned King James I of England, thus unifying the crowns of England and Scotland. James believed that he ruled by divine right.

Not long after James began to reign in London, Puritan ministers pressed him to allow a further reformation of the Church of England. James thought these could be the first steps to establishing a Presbyterian form of church government independent from the king like they had in Scotland. James refused any compromise with the Puritans. "No bishop, no king!" he said. He viewed their efforts to purify the church as disloyalty. He insisted on strict uniformity of worship in the kingdom. "I will make them conform themselves," James said, "or else I will harass them out of the land, or else do worse."

James and his bishops ejected many Puritans from their churches, if they refused to conform. His efforts to force the rule of bishops on the Presbyterians in Scotland met with resistance.

CHARLES I (King of England and Scotland, 1625-1649) thought, as his father did, that he ruled by divine right. He tried to exercise absolute power regardless of what the parliaments of England or Scotland thought. Eventually, the king dissolved the English Parliament and tried to rule without them. With the Archbishop of Canterbury, William Laud, Charles sought to control the churches of both kingdoms. He wanted to replace the Reformed theology of the Puritans and the Covenanters with an Arminian theology, emphasizing high church sacramental worship that smacked of Roman Catholicism.

Laud ejected nonconformist ministers from their churches and Puritan professors from their colleges. The authorities hauled Puritans before secret courts and cast them into prison. In 1637, Charles and Laud forced on Scotland the use of a new worship book full of ceremonies and prayers that most Scots thought were not biblical. Scots rose up in defiance. Thousands of people across Scotland signed the National Covenant which proclaimed the liberty of the Scottish church from interference from the crown. Charles raised an army to put them down. The Scots organized an army of Covenanters. When Charles called the English Parliament into session to raise funds to wage war against Scotland, Puritans in Parliament demanded reforms. They wanted an end to the king's meddling in the church, and they protested his ignoring the Parliament's constitutional rights.

The conflict erupted into civil war, pitting the forces of the king against Parliament's army. Eventually, Charles's forces were defeated. The English Parliament tried and convicted him of high treason, and executed him in January 1649.

CHARLES II (King of England and Scotland, 1660-1685)—For eleven years, the English Parliament, controlled by Puritans, ruled without a king. In 1660, Charles II, son of the executed Charles I, returned from exile and was crowned king. Charles swore an oath to the Scots and the English that he would not interfere with their churches. But not long after coming to the throne, his government moved to crush Puritan and the Covenanter influence.

Like his father before him, he sought to enforce religious conformity, making compulsory the use of the prayers and ceremonies of the Book of Common Prayer. Any unauthorized gathering of five or more people for worship, prayer, or Bible study was strictly forbidden under penalty of fines or imprisonment. In Scotland, he outlawed Presbyterian church government and installed bishops to rule the church. Many Covenanters and Puritans believed they had to make a choice—obey God or the king. Thousands of ministers in England and Scotland refused to conform to the king's demands and were ejected from their pulpits. The prisons filled with nonconformists and Covenanters. The Scots suffered the worse. The government hanged several thousand Covenanters for worshiping Christ in ways not approved by the Crown.

JAMES II (King of England and Scotland, 1685-1688), the brother of Charles II, was a Roman Catholic who continued the persecution of Covenanters and Puritans. Fearful that James planned to return the Church of England to Roman Catholicism, English noblemen rose up against him. They asked William III, Prince of Orange (the grandson of Charles I), to bring his Dutch army to Britain. When William landed his troops, leading English politicians and generals welcomed him as a liberator. James II fled the country. William and his wife Mary (James II's daughter) began to rule England and Scotland in 1688. The persecution of Puritans and Covenanters by the Crown ended.

1

THOMAS CARTWRIGHT

Father of English Presbyterianism

(1535–1603)

On December 11, 1573, the Bishop of London signed an arrest warrant for Thomas Cartwright, a man that Queen Elizabeth considered a traitor and a rebel. "To all mayors, sheriffs, constables and to all other officers of the Queen's Majesty," the warrant stated, "we command you in the Queen's name that you assist in every way possible to apprehend Thomas Cartwright, wherever he might be within the realm. If you fail to do this with all diligence, you will face the utmost peril."

Who was this Cartwright and what had he done to make his arrest so urgent? Thomas Cartwright, a minister and theologian was the Lady Margaret Professor of Divinity at the University of Cambridge, one of the most prestigious academic posts in the kingdom. He got up at 3 o'clock every morning to spend several hours communing with God in prayer and Bible reading before sunrise. Cartwright brought the Scriptures to life to the students who crowded in for his lectures on the Bible. They reported that listening to Cartwright was like hearing a prophet of old bringing them the very words of God. "Preach the glorious gospel of our blessed God," he urged the young men.

Whenever Cartwright preached at Great St. Mary's Church, the large university church in the center of Cambridge, the pews and aisles filled long before the service began. The church wardens took down the windows so that the multitudes who stood outside could hear him. He called them to turn from their sins, believe and live for God. "Come to God in repentance," he preached, "and to our Lord Jesus Christ in faith."

Cartwright defended the English Reformation and worked to reform the Church of England according to the Word of God. Those who wanted to reform or purify the church were called Puritans, and Cartwright was foremost among them. However, the Puritans disagreed about how the church should be governed. Some Puritans accepted the Church of England's episcopal system where a hierarchy of archbishops and bishops ruled the church. Others thought that each local church should be independent, able to completely run its own affairs. Through Cartwright's study of the New Testament, he came to believe that the church should be governed by its own ministers and elders, freely chosen by each congregation. He taught that church doctrine, worship and discipline should be decided according to the Scriptures by an assembly of ministers and ruling elders, not by bishops appointed by the Crown. Cartwright envisioned a Presbyterian form of church government for England where oversight of the church rested in the hands of presbyters, another name for elders.

He also argued that the Book of Common Prayer, the worship guide of the church, should not require ministers and people to participate in worship ceremonies not taught in the Bible. But the queen and her archbishop demanded, under penalty of fines and imprisonment, that everyone bow whenever Jesus' name was mentioned in the service, face east during the Scripture readings and kneel for the Lord's Supper. Cartwright and other Puritan reformers did not mind if some chose to do these things in worship, but they did not want them forced on everyone.

The Archbishop of Canterbury said that Cartwright's opinions deceived so many in the kingdom that he ordered his clergy "to beat them out of the heads of the people."

In 1570, the archbishop demanded that the chancellor of Cambridge University remove Cartwright. "The youth of the university frequent his lectures in great numbers and therefore are in danger of being poisoned by him," the archbishop wrote.

"I have taught nothing which did not naturally arise from the Bible passage on which I was lecturing," Cartwright told the chancellor. "I do not deny that I have said the Church of England has deviated from the apostolic church. But I said this in so candid and modest a way that none but ignorant or malicious persons could find fault."

Many leading professors in the university defended Cartwright to the chancellor, praising his upright life and his knowledge of Latin, Greek, and Hebrew. "If you have conceived any bad opinion of him," they wrote, "dismiss it from your mind. Give credit to us who are well acquainted with his character, religion, and learning, rather than to anonymous slanderers destitute of truth and candor."

Despite the pleas of students and faculty members, the chancellor, under pressure from the Archbishop of Canterbury, expelled Cartwright from the university. The queen's government denied him a license to preach. At the same time, they ejected hundreds of Puritan ministers from their pulpits in England.

"You exhort us to submit ourselves to good order which we have always done and are still ready to do," Cartwright wrote in defense of himself and other persecuted reformers. "You call us to join you in preaching the Word of God, but you have stopped our mouths and will not permit us to preach."

For two years, Cartwright lived in London with friends. He ministered to people in small groups, and tutored students, and wrote. Cartwright wrote pamphlets, urging church officials to require of ministers and parishioners only what is taught in the Scriptures. "We do not intend to take away the power of the civil magistrate," Cartwright wrote, "but that Christ may rule the church by the scepter of His Word."

The authorities banned his writings. Citizens who owned his books could be thrown in jail. The Bishop of London demanded that printers and booksellers turn over any copies of Cartwright's works. Although thousands of copies of Cartwright's books circulated in London, very few were turned in to the government.

The queen's council branded Cartwright an enemy of the state and issued a warrant for his arrest. "We shall root out Puritanism and the supporters of it!" Queen Elizabeth declared.

"I have the Word of God for my warrant," Cartwright said.

In order to evade the clutches of the queen, Cartwright escaped England for Europe. He traveled to Geneva where he met Theodore Beza, the great reformer and successor to John Calvin. Beza recognized the brilliance of Cartwright's mind. "I think the sun does not see a more learned man," Beza said of him.

Eventually, Thomas Cartwright settled in Antwerp where he preached to English merchants and others who had fled England to escape religious persecution. Under Cartwright's direction, they organized their church government and worship according to the Scriptures. "Try the weight of every argument," he taught his flock, "not by the deceitful scales of men, but by the authority of the Word of God."

The church thrived and so did Cartwright. In Antwerp, he met and married Alice Stubbs. They had several children.

After many years abroad, Cartwright's health broke down. Doctors recommended that breathing his native air might restore his strength—so in 1585, he returned to England. No sooner had he landed in the kingdom than he was arrested and thrown into prison. After Cartwright suffered a few months in jail, influential friends won his release, but church officials refused to grant him a license to preach. The Earl of Leicester, a supporter of the Puritans, appointed Cartwright to head the hospital that he had founded at Warwick. The hospital chapel was not under the control of the bishop, so Cartwright could preach there.

However, church officials kept harassing him. Cartwright's most determined foe was John Whitgift. Whitgift had once been a friend and fellow reformer with Cartwright at Cambridge. But when Whitgift faced the queen's ire for his views, he apologized and became a fierce persecutor of the Puritans. As the queen's man, Whitgift advanced rapidly. In 1583, Elizabeth made him the Archbishop of Canterbury, the ruling prelate of the Church of England. Whitgift used the power of his office to launch a crusade against the Puritans. "I would rather live and die in a prison," he said, "than grant any indulgence to Puritans!"

Despite the hatred heaped upon him by church leaders, Cartwright strove to think the best of everyone, including his persecutors. "He could not endure to hear even his adversaries reproached," a friend said of Cartwright. "If any person spoke disrespectfully of them in his presence, he would sharply rebuke him, saying, 'It is a Christian's duty to pray for his enemies and not reproach them.'"

In 1590, Archbishop Whitgift hauled Cartwright before the Court of High Commission. The court claimed he had called the Church of England "anti-Christian and unlawful." They stated that he had no right to serve as minister and practice Presbyterian church government in Antwerp without the queen's permission. In addition, they made the ridiculous claims that he had threatened to excommunicate the queen and that he had stabbed a man with a knife. "I am charged," Cartwright told the court, "with things which I not only never did, but which never so much as entered into my thoughts."

Many prominent people wrote the court to defend Cartwright's character against the absurd attacks. But the court cast him into the Fleet, a notorious prison on the banks of the Fleet River in London, infamous for its cruelty to prisoners. While Cartwright languished in a dark cell, torn from his family and ministry, Archbishop Whitgift basked in splendor at Lambeth Palace, catered to by an army of servants.

Living month after month in a damp, cold prison caused his ankles, knees, and elbows to swell and throb. Severe pain in his back radiated down his legs. "I was scarcely able to bear the weight of my own clothes," Cartwright said.

During this time, one of his children died, but being locked away, Cartwright was unable to comfort his wife and children. He asked to be released on bail, a common practice at the time, but he was denied.

Some high officials recoiled at the persecution of Puritans by the queen and her archbishop. Whitgift said he would release Cartwright and other Puritan reformers if they swore an oath that the queen was the undisputed governor of the church and acknowledged that "everything in the Book of Common Prayer was according to the Word of God." Cartwright and his fellow Puritan sufferers could not agree to take any oath that made the Queen of England as powerful in the Church of England as the Pope was in the Church of Rome.

Finally, after two years in Fleet prison, the queen's council released Cartwright. He returned to Warwick Hospital where he taught the Scriptures to the patients and their families. Several times a week, people crowded the chapel to hear him preach. In his old age, he was permitted to preach outside the hospital. Once, he was invited to preach at Great St. Mary's Church in Cambridge. It had been many years since he had preached there. Students, faculty and townspeople jammed the church to hear the famous old Puritan. It was said that a number of professors "ran like boys in the street to obtain places in the church."

Cartwright died on December 27, 1603, at the age of 68. The morning of his death, he spent two hours in prayer, and found himself overwhelmed by the joy of the Lord. He told his wife, "God gave me a glimpse of heaven."

2

EDWARD DERING

Fearless Puritan Preacher

(c. 1540–1576)

In February 1570, Edward Dering, a young minister, stood to preach before Queen Elizabeth and her royal court. For a dozen years, the queen, as head of both church and state had steered the English church down a middle path between Roman Catholics and Reformers. Under Elizabeth, the Church of England reestablished its independence from the pope, but the church's worship remained strongly influenced by Roman Catholicism.

The Church of England was in a sorry state. The bishops, allied with the queen, resisted reform. Poorly trained ministers, ignorant of the Scriptures, couldn't deliver a biblical sermon. Many men became ministers for the steady income and the free time to pursue their own pleasures. People came to church because it was against the law not to. Those who failed to attend worship on Sunday faced fines or imprisonment. During services the bored congregation paid little attention to the preacher's message. In most churches, they wouldn't have learned anything of value if they had. The Puritans wanted to reform the church according to the teaching of the Bible and train godly ministers to preach the good news of Jesus Christ. But Elizabeth had no intention of letting the Puritans change the church. She believed it would weaken her authority and cause divisions in the land.

Edward Dering, a university lecturer and the finest scholar of Greek in the kingdom, was a rising star in the Church of England. The Archbishop of Canterbury called him "the greatest learned man in England." His biblical preaching in the colleges and churches of Cambridge gained a large following of students and townspeople.

As Dering entered the pulpit of the queen's chapel, he knew that if he pleased Elizabeth, she would reward him with a plum office in the church and set him on a path of influence and wealth. Before he arrived at the royal chapel, a courtier told him, "He that will speak safely to a king must speak with silken words."

But Dering's heart ached for the English people whom he saw as starving sheep without a shepherd. Lazy ministers who cared only for themselves and not for their flocks made his blood boil. He complained that many ministers "are clothed in scarlet while their flocks perish for cold; and while they eat delicious food, their people are faint with a most miserable hunger."

Dering knew that most English ministers did not understand the life, death and resurrection of Christ. Their sermons came more from the ideas of the classical philosophers than from the good news of the Bible. "They use the pulpit like a philosopher's chair," he lamented.

His conscience would not allow him to win the queen's favor with smooth talk, telling her what she wanted to hear. "I do not love to speak fair," he told a friend, "for I see what mischief is bred from flattery and deceitful praises."

In his sermon to the queen, he traced examples of faithful rulers in the Bible who used their power to advance the kingdom of God. He told her that everything she had was a gift from God who had protected her kingdom and showered her with mercy. Such blessings, he said, should call forth gratitude and obedience. "I beseech your Majesty to hearken," he told her. "I will speak nothing according to man. But that which I will speak shall be out of the mouth of the Lord, obeying it shall be your safeguard and the health of your kingdom."

He reminded the queen that Christ called ministers to be the light of the world, but that most English pastors lived in spiritual

EDWARD DERING

"Throughout the sermon, the queen sat fuming."

darkness. Called to feed biblical truth to their flocks, ministers had none to give them. They were supposed to be messengers of glad tidings, but they didn't understand the good news. "Have pity on your poor subjects," he implored her.

Dering challenged the queen to use her power to root out corrupt and incompetent ministers. "Look upon your clergymen!" he told her. "Some are ruffians, some hawkers and hunters, some dicers and carders, some blind guides and cannot see, some dumb dogs and will not bark."

Then he chastised the queen for failing to do anything about the Christ-less ministers in her realm. "And yet you," Dering said, "while all these abominations are committed, you at whose hands God will require it, you sit still and are careless, and let men do as they please—well contented to leave it all alone. May the Lord increase the gifts of his Holy Spirit in you that from faith to faith you may grow continually until you are as zealous as good King David to work His will."

Throughout the sermon the queen sat fuming. She had never been preached to like that before. Before Dering left the royal court, Elizabeth banned him from preaching anywhere in her kingdom. He returned to Cambridge, grieving that he was prevented from preaching, but he believed that he had done the right thing. "Though I bear the loss of worldly things," he told his brother, "yet by the grace of Christ, I will never lose a good conscience. And though they are angry with me, I will not stop praying for them and commit my cause unto God."

Some Puritans criticized Dering for being too blunt and harsh with the queen. Others admired his courage and compared him to John Knox, the fearless Scottish reformer.

He continued to prepare his college students for the ministry. "Study the Scripture," he told them, "read books, be able to reason in your faith, and above all, have a lively feeling of God."

Dering taught them that their sermons must be based on clearly explained Bible passages. Everything that you say and do, he told them, must be "grounded on Holy Scripture."

Despite the queen's anger at his message, he kept exposing the deplorable state of England's clergymen. "There was never a nation," he said, "which had so ignorant ministers."

When Thomas Cartwright, a renowned Puritan scholar at Cambridge, was expelled from the university, Dering boldly led the fight to have him reinstated even though it jeopardized his own position. Christ and his cause meant far more to him than his standing in the world. "I weigh not all the world a feather," he said.

The preaching ban was a terrible hardship to Dering. For like the apostle Paul, Dering said, "Woe unto me if I preach not the gospel!"

He loved to point his hearers to Jesus Christ. "The forgiveness of our sins is only in the precious blood of Jesus Christ," he preached. "Expect no salvation but in the righteousness of Jesus Christ. For we all stand in need of the grace of God."

"Our flesh, the world, and the devil they are too strong for us," Dering proclaimed, "but blessed be the Lord God who has given us victory in Jesus Christ."

He challenged believers to live a holy life. "Let there not be a day but shall strengthen our faith," Dering preached, "that we may be glad we are one day nearer the presence of God than we were before."

But he taught Christians not to be too discouraged by their sins and weak faith. "It is necessary that you should know your sin," he said, "or you could not understand how great is your redemption."

"For what were the Romans, Corinthians, Ephesians, Galatians, and all others whom the Spirit named saints and holy ones?" Dering asked. "Was not their faith as frail and weak as ours is? Yet the Spirit called them saints and so He calls us also. Fear not—you are anointed of the Lord and you shall not fall."

"Set your minds on things above where Christ is seated at the Father's right hand," Dering told his hearers, reminding them that Christians had a far greater treasure in Christ stored up in heaven. "Knit that truth fast to all the thoughts of your heart and never forget it," he said. "It should give you more pleasure in one day of your life than you could find in a thousand years without it. All the men of the world who feel their pleasures in this life shall perish when you shall abide. They shall mourn when you shall rejoice because they have forgotten the living God whom you have loved."

After many months of suffering under the preaching ban, he wrote Queen Elizabeth a respectful letter asking her to grant him permission to preach again. But Dering did not apologize for his sermon. He told the queen that he was being faithful to his calling as a minister to tell her the truth. "Duty and necessity compelled me," he wrote. "I will not betray the truth of God."

Eventually, Elizabeth lifted the preaching ban, and he became a preacher at St. Paul's Cathedral in London. He preached a series of sermons there on the epistle to the Hebrews. "I will show you the argument of the whole epistle," he said, "that only in Jesus Christ is the forgiveness of our sins."

"Now let us praise Almighty God our heavenly Father," Dering preached, "who has so loved us that he gave his only begotten Son to lead us in the way of truth to save us from the bondage of death and to sacrifice his own body for the ransom of our sins."

Crowds flocked to the great cathedral to hear him explain the Scriptures clearly and powerfully. Even though he was the most popular preacher in London, the queen still disapproved of his preaching. Then one morning as he was about to preach, a church official came to him and said, "In the name of her majesty the queen, you are forbidden to preach."

Shortly thereafter, constables arrested Dering and forced him to stand trial for sedition and heresy. Although the court acquitted him of the charges, it stripped him of his church office and forbade him to preach. "I am content to bear it," he wrote to his brother, "God will supply my needs when I am able to do nothing."

Soon he came down with tuberculosis which filled his lungs with fluid and made it hard to breathe. A constant high fever and persistent cough kept him from sleeping. Throughout his painful ordeal, he remained cheerful and full of faith in God. "Afflictions, diseases, sickness, and grief are nothing but part of the portion which God has allotted to us in this world," he said. "To those that love God all things are for the best."

After hearing that a Christian friend was suffering from a painful illness, he sent her a letter from his sickbed. "One day God will make these mortal bodies like the glorious body of his dear and well beloved Son," he wrote. "This we know and in this we are comforted."

As Dering's life was ebbing away, a group of his minister friends came to visit. "I hope your mind is filled with holy meditations," one said.

"Poor wretch and miserable man that I am," Dering answered, "the least of all the saints, and the greatest of sinners, yet by the eye of faith I believe in and look upon Christ my Savior."

His friends tried to make it easier for him to speak by propping him up on a pillow. As sunlight from the window lit up his pale face, he said, "I bless God that I feel so much inward joy and comfort in my soul. If I had to choose whether to die or live, I would a thousand times rather choose death than life, if it is the holy will of God."

Not long after the ministers left, Edward Dering died. He was just thirty-six years old.

His example of fearless preaching and his published writings and sermons inspired the Puritans who came after him. The famous Scottish Covenanter Samuel Rutherford said that Edward Dering was one of the authors who influenced him the most.

3

RICHARD GREENHAM

Diligent Country Pastor

(c. 1540–1594)

In 1570, Richard Greenham left his comfortable and happy life as a teacher at Pembroke College to pastor an English country parish in Dry Dayton, a village five miles from Cambridge. Dry Drayton had less than 300 residents, mostly poor farmers and laborers.

Greenham's life experience varied greatly from his flock's. He was a highly educated university instructor who had spent years studying the Scriptures, philosophy, theology, rhetoric, and classical languages. Most of his parishioners could not read or write, and very few owned a Bible. Although his parish of the Church of England used the Book of Common Prayer for worship, the people had never been taught the Word of God. Steeped in ignorance and superstition, they knew more about Robin Hood than Jesus Christ.

Like other country pastors of his day, Greenham found his congregation disinterested in the things of God. In order to avoid being fined by the government, most people came to church on Sunday, but during services they fidgeted, gossiped, joked or fell asleep. Many arrived late and some walked out early. Greenham had his work cut out for him to teach his parishioners the good news of Jesus Christ.

Rolling up his sleeves, he went right to work—preaching, teaching and visiting. Almost every day, Greenham called upon a few of his people in their cottages, making a point of visiting every home in the parish several times a year. A parishioner observed that it was Greenham's habit "to walk out into the fields and to talk with his neighbors as they were at the plow."

He worried about the spiritual state of his people. "They think either that there is no God," Greenham said, "or else that He is not as fearful and merciful as the Bible describes Him to be."

Setting a grueling schedule for himself, he preached twice on Sunday and four mornings a week before the farmers began working their fields. On Sunday afternoons, he taught the youth from a catechism that he had written to explain the faith to them. To prepare for his demanding preaching and teaching schedule, Greenham rose each day at four o'clock in the morning to pray, study the Bible and prepare sermons. His fervent prayers, often accompanied with sighs and groans, made his wife wonder at times if her husband was coming down with a painful illness.

Greenham preached about Christ, salvation and the Christian life. "Let us labor to have Christ crucified in our hearts," he told them. Many of his sermons proclaimed the law of God and called his hearers to live holy lives. "I preached God's commandments," he said, "to drive men out of themselves and send them to Christ."

"Every day must have a day's increase in godliness," he taught.

He preached with such passion and energy, one man reported, "that his shirt would usually be as wet with sweating, as if it had been drenched in water."

Like many of his fellow Puritan preachers, Greenham strove to keep the eyes of his congregation on heaven. "Paradise is our native country," he taught, "and in this world we are as exiles and strangers."

God uses all the trials and disappointments of our lives, he told them, "to fit and prepare us for the kingdom of heaven."

One of God's greatest gifts to his children, Greenham believed, was the Lord's Day—one day each week God set aside for people to rest from their daily toils and to worship. Greenham called the Christian Sabbath "the feeding day of the soul."

He taught his flock that the Lord's Day was not only for worship and prayer, but also for loving one's neighbor and helping the poor. "The Lord's Sabbath is not a day of knowledge alone, but of love," he said. Greenham wrote a popular book on the Christian Sabbath that influenced English-speaking Christians for years.

If his parishioners opened their hearts to the Holy Spirit as they listened to the preaching, Greenham told them, God would change their hearts. "Run to every sermon," he said. "Turn all that you remember into a prayer."

But despite all his urgings, the effect of his messages quickly left his people. He called their resistance to the teaching of God's Word "sermon sickness." "As soon as they are out of the church doors," Greenham said, "they forget what they heard and so return to their former life again."

If his sermons did not lead them to Christ, then he determined to do it through one-on-one conversation. His kindness, sympathy, and wise counsel attracted people to him like moths to a flame. Soon distressed folks from within his parish and beyond came to him with their troubles and doubts. Puritan pastors strove to be physicians of the soul through their preaching and counseling, and Greenham set the standard for many. One minister said that Greenham had a great empathy for those in spiritual torment and felt for them "as if he had been afflicted with them."

Knowing that true peace of mind came only to those who had a living faith in Christ; Greenham confronted the distressed with their sin and their need for a Savior. "No sin is so great," Greenham assured them, "but in Christ it is pardonable."

"O be of good comfort," he told those overcome with sadness, "we hold Christ by faith, and not by feeling."

A fellow minister said that Greenham abundantly applied to individuals "the oil of the gospel and its sweet promises."

No matter the time of day or night, Greenham gladly gave his undivided attention to anyone who sought his aid. Once, a man apologized for taking up too much of his time. Greenham replied with a wide smile, "I live for this."

The workers of his parish barely earned enough money to survive. Greenham used his income and his influence to make life better for them. He gave generously to any needy person who came to his door. The inmates at the prison on Castle Hill in Cambridge knew that whenever Greenham came by, he would give them some money to ease their pains. If he heard that a merchant had cheated anyone in the market, he publicly exposed it. Part of his income came from the grain grown on church land. He convinced the wealthiest landlords in the area to create a community granary where, during times of high prices, the poor could buy grain for their families at half the market price. Greenham was one of the largest donors to the granary.

"Relieve the needy," he taught his parishioners, "and help the afflicted."

Greenham's reputation for preaching and counseling led to many offers from larger churches that promised to pay him a much higher salary. "Leave," his Cambridge friends urged him, "stop wasting your talents on those hard-hearted country folk."

But Greenham stayed put, saying, "If I ever took a call to a different church, I would not accept a penny more than I am paid in Dry Drayton."

Realizing that the well-being of the church's future rested in the hands of young pastors, Greenham helped to prepare Cambridge students for the ministry by bringing one young man at a time to Dry Drayton for an internship. They lodged and ate meals in his home and worked shoulder to shoulder with him in the parish. Greenham believed that it was a biblical practice for older ministers to train younger ones, and he urged good pastors to do it. "Joshua ministered to Moses," Greenham said, "Elisha to Elijah, Samuel to Eli, the disciples to Christ, and Timothy to Paul . . . therefore every godly learned minister should train up some young scholar."

These were days of great controversy in the church. Greenham's friend, Thomas Cartwright, had been driven out of Cambridge and lived in exile in Europe for speaking out for reforms. His colleague, Edward Dering, had been banned from preaching. The Acts of Uniformity pressed by the queen and adopted by Parliament attempted to force every minister in the Church of England to perform ceremonies and wear clerical clothing that many considered to be unbiblical. Greenham agreed with Cartwright and Dering on most of the issues. He refused to use ceremonies that he thought to be unscriptural, but he approached the controversies meekly. Above all, he wanted the freedom to preach the good news of Jesus Christ.

Greenham believed that many of the divisions in the Church of England were caused by ministers who failed to love their flocks and one another. "Be gentle and courteous," he advised pastors. One minister said that in all Greenham's disagreements with other clergymen, "He labored to retain love."

"In his holy ministry," a close friend said, "he was ever careful to avoid all occasions of offense."

When a young minister told Greenham that he planned to preach against the false practices in the church, Greenham told him, "preach faith and repentance from sin first."

Heated debates erupted in the church about whether the Church of England should have an episcopal or a presbyterian form of church government. "Many meddle and stir much about a new church government," he wrote, "who are senseless and barren in the doctrine of the new birth."

What good is it, Greenham wondered, for a minister to be zealous for a system of church government "and yet know not himself to be a new creature in Jesus Christ?"

Despite years of tireless efforts, his congregation largely resisted his teaching. One Puritan writer, looking back on Greenham's ministry, said that despite all his counsel, tears, prayers, charity, visits, and sermons, "his parish remained ignorant and obstinate."

At times, he wondered if he should leave the ministry all together since God did not seem to be blessing his labors.

In 1591, after twenty-one years of hard work that appeared to have little impact on his flock, Greenham left his rural village for London. Before he left Dry Drayton, he told the minister sent to replace him, "God bless you, and send you more fruit of your labors than I have had; for I perceive no good wrought by my ministry on any but one family."

Greenham had planted and watered the seed of the gospel. He had showed how to be a faithful minister. A generation of Christian pastors, inspired by his example, strove to follow in his steps.

4

WILLIAM PERKINS

Plain and Powerful Preacher

(1558–1602)

Late one afternoon around the year 1577, William Perkins staggered home. The heavy-set, blond-haired student of Christ's College in Cambridge had spent the last several hours getting drunk with his friends in an alehouse. This was not unusual. He spent most mornings studying and most afternoons and evenings drinking. Although Perkins was a brilliant student, he had turned away from the Christianity of his upbringing and had become arrogant and foul-mouthed. At Cambridge, William Perkins poured his energy into two things—mathematics and wild living.

Reeking of alcohol and feeling queasy, he stumbled along the streets of the university town in search of his front door. Near his home, he passed by a neighbor woman who was scolding her young child. "Hold your tongue," the mother warned, "or I will give you to drunken Perkins over there."

When William Perkins found his room and fell into bed, the words of the woman in the street swirled around and around in his head. "So," he said to himself, "I am known in the neighborhood as a drunken fool."

The woman's remark cut through him like a sword thrust. For the first time in his life, he saw the evil in his heart and the folly of his ways. Unable to drive the thought of his guilt before God out of his head, he started to read the Bible and go to church, hoping that would relieve his stricken conscience. At first, this did not ease his mind because he realized all the more that he was a lost sinner—hopeless unless God showed him mercy. Before long, after hearing many sermons from Puritan preachers, he knew what he had to do. Perkins turned to Jesus Christ for the forgiveness of his sins, and he asked his Savior for a new heart.

As day is to night, so was the new Perkins to the old. He stopped drinking and started praying. He stopped carousing and started serving. To his surprise, he found his selfishness shrinking and his love for others growing. Not long after, he believed that God was calling him to become a minister. Abandoning mathematics, he devoted himself to the study of the Scriptures and theology.

Cambridge was the birthplace of Puritanism in England. The Puritans taught that sinners are saved only by believing in Christ and His sacrifice on the cross. They also taught that Christians are called to obey God's commandments and live holy lives. The old Perkins despised the Puritans. He thought that they didn't want people to have any fun. But now William Perkins embraced Puritan teaching with all his heart. He devoured the writings of Thomas Cartwright and other Puritan leaders who emphasized that salvation was a gift of God's free grace by faith in Christ. They taught that only the Bible should guide believers how to worship and live.

When he completed his studies, Perkins was ordained as a minister in the Church of England and he was chosen to be a fellow of Christ's College. The responsibilities of a college fellow included lecturing and tutoring students. Fellows also preached in chapel and counseled students. Perkins did not preach like most ministers did in that day. Wanting to impress their audiences, they used flowery language and filled their sermons with lots of quotes from poets and philosophers. Perkins used plain words to explain the meaning of a Bible passage and challenged his hearers to believe and obey God's Word. Soon students packed the college chapel to hear him preach.

William Perkins's cheerfulness and kindness made him easy to approach. He had a special knack for listening to people and then applying the good news of Jesus to each one. Seeing his care for others, many students came to him for private spiritual counsel. "He had a spirit of sympathy for perishing sinners," a friend of Perkins said.

Through Perkins and other Puritan preachers, a great awakening of faith broke out in Cambridge—hundreds of students put their trust in Jesus Christ, and many dedicated their lives to proclaiming forgiveness in Christ. But his concern for souls burst beyond the privileged scholars of the colleges to the poor and despised of the town. His heart went out to the prisoners languishing without hope in the jail cells of Cambridge Castle. Like his Savior, he longed to preach freedom to the captives.

Perkins convinced the jailor to bring any inmates willing to hear him to a large meeting room in the Shire-house next door to the prison. Every Sunday, William Perkins preached to the prisoners who came bound in iron chains and clothed in filthy rags. He began by explaining in simple terms the sinfulness of each human heart. He said that every sinner was a rebel against God and deserved the punishment of hell. Then he told them that Jesus would fully forgive all the sins of anyone who believed in Him. Some people in Cambridge mocked Perkins and called him "the jail bird chaplain." But by the grace of God, many prisoners believed in Jesus Christ. "He was the happy instrument of converting many of them to God," one minister said of Perkins, "freeing them from the captivity of sin which was their worst bondage."

Word spread about the remarkable effects of Perkins's preaching. People marveled that even hardened criminals turned to God. Before long, townspeople flocked to the Shire-house, and stood shoulder-to shoulder with the shackled prisoners to hear Perkins preach the good news of Christ. Many of them put their trust in Jesus.

At that time, the government put people to death for many different crimes—hanging them from a tall wooden gallows in a public place for all to see. Watching executions was a popular form of gruesome entertainment. Perkins went to hangings not to watch someone die, but to tell the condemned criminals about Christ's love. One day, a young man who had been sentenced to death, nervously climbed the ladder of the gallows. When he reached the top, he stared at the hangman's noose. His body shook and his face turned a ghastly pale. He looked as if he were half-dead already. "What is the matter with you?" Perkins called out to the man. "Are you afraid to die?"

The crowd grew silent. First they looked at Perkins and then they looked up to the quivering man on the gallows.

"No," said the trembling prisoner, "I am afraid of a far worse thing."

"Is that so," Perkins replied. "Come down here again and you will see what God's grace can do to strengthen you."

The hangman permitted the condemned man to go down the ladder. Perkins met him at the bottom rung and took him by the hand. At the foot of the ladder, they knelt in the dirt together. Perkins prayed aloud. When he prayed that sin was a great offense against a holy God which called for banishment to hell, the prisoner burst into tears. Seeing that the man understood that he was a guilty sinner, Perkins prayed. "The Lord Jesus Christ is the Savior of all penitent and believing sinners. Look to Him who stretches out His hand of mercy to save you in your distress and deliver you from the powers of darkness."

Right then and there, the condemned man put his trust in Jesus Christ. Immediately, his face brightened. His sobs of fear turned to tears of joy. Some of the bystanders raised their hands and praised God aloud for His mercy to the poor fellow. "He rose from his knees cheerfully," an eyewitness said later, "and went up the ladder again so comforted. He took his death with such patience and calm, as if he actually saw himself delivered from hell and heaven opened to receive his soul."

In 1584, Perkins became the minister of Saint Andrew's Church in Cambridge while he remained a fellow at Christ's College. He served at St. Andrew's for the rest of his life. Students and professors, townspeople and country folk, packed the pews of the church every Lord's Day to hear him. His messages were deep enough to challenge university scholars, but also understandable to poor beggars. Through his straightforward preaching, he awakened sinners to the horrible judgment that they would face if they did not believe in Christ. A minister said that when Perkins spoke about hell, it made his hearers' "hearts fall down and their hairs stand upright."

Perkins, like all Puritans, stressed a close personal walk with the Savior. Perkins grew in the grace and practice of daily looking to Christ and obeying Him moment by moment. The godly character of his life became well known. It was said, "He lived his sermons." Even those who disagreed with him were forced to admit that Perkins was a holy man.

During this time, William Perkins began to write books—books on theology and commentaries on the New Testament. His book on preaching explained how to prepare a biblical sermon that set the standard for Puritan preachers to follow. He was crippled in his right hand so he wrote with his left. He used to put on the title page of all his writings: "You are a minister of the Word: Mind your business."

Through his preaching and writing, Perkins became the most influential Puritan minister in the kingdom. His books outsold nearly all other Christian authors. They were translated into many languages. Perkins got very little money from the sale of his books, and his salary from St. Andrew's Church was small. Despite the financial strain on his large family, he turned down many offers from higher-paying ministries out of love for his Cambridge flock.

Perkins wanted to see the Church of England follow the teachings of the Bible alone in all of its beliefs, worship, and practices. He wrote about the need to reform the church in accordance with the Word of God. But his ideas got him into trouble.

Queen Elizabeth I did not like the Puritans or their views. She saw the Puritans as troublemakers whose ideas would upset the unity of the church. The queen demanded that all her subjects conform to the same religious beliefs and practices. When the queen's government began to expel Puritan ministers from their pulpits and imprison some, Perkins spoke out against it. Several times he was hauled into court to face accusations that he was a rebel against the queen and her bishops.

At one appearance before the High Court, Perkins defended himself against the accusation that he was disloyal to the government and the church. After explaining his beliefs, he said, "These things I have said to show that I do not despise authority. If this satisfies you, God be praised, but if not, God's will be done."

However, Perkins's fame as a scholar, his unimpeachable character and his many supporters kept him out of prison.

In 1602, at the age of 44, Perkins fell gravely ill. In those days, they did not have good medicines to relieve pain. Sick people often suffered horribly. His final illness brought excruciating pain. When a friend came to visit him on his sickbed, he prayed that God would free Perkins of his pain. "Stop!" Perkins interrupted his friend. "Do not pray so, but pray that the Lord will give me faith and patience, and then let Him lay on me what He pleases."

He died a few days later. But William Perkins's godly influence lived on through his students and through his writings. John Cotton, a Cambridge graduate and a famous Puritan minister in New England, said that Perkins's ministry was "one good reason why so many excellent preachers came out of Cambridge in England."

5

ANDREW MELVILLE

Courageous in the Cause of Christ

(1545–1622)

In 1582, a group of Scottish ministers stood before King James VI. They presented a petition complaining of the king's interference with the Church of Scotland. The main spokesman was Andrew Melville. A friend had warned him not to go. "The king and his noblemen are furious with you," he told him. "You might be killed."

"I am not afraid in the cause of Christ," Melville answered.

After they read the petition to the king and his council, one of the royal advisors leapt to his feet and cried out, "Who dares sign these treasonable articles?"

"We dare," Andrew Melville said, stepping forward and signing his name to the petition. One by one the other ministers signed their names also.

This wasn't the first time that Melville had challenged the king or his men. As a long-time champion of independence for the Church of Scotland from the dictates of the crown, he had been summoned to the royal court before to account for his actions. Once, James's chief official told him that it was an act of treason for church leaders to meet without the king's permission. "Then Christ and his apostles must have been guilty of treason," Melville answered, "for they met with thousands without asking permission of the magistrates."

The official grew red in the face and shouted, "There will never be peace in this country until half a dozen of you preachers are hanged or banished."

"Listen, sir," Melville said, "It doesn't matter to me whether I rot in the air or in the ground. I am ready to give my life at the pleasure of my God. But you have no power to hang or exile God's truth."

Although Melville was a minister and preached regularly, he spent most of his time as the head of the University of St. Andrews. A gifted scholar in Greek, Hebrew, Latin, and theology, Melville almost single-handedly revived the quality of university education in Scotland. His fame as a scholar and teacher spread far and wide, and students came from all over Europe to study under him.

As a young man, Melville left Scotland to learn from the finest professors in France and he taught for ten years in French universities and in Geneva, Switzerland. He was in Geneva in 1572, when the French king ordered the slaughter of thousands of Protestants in France. Many survivors of the St. Bartholomew's Day Massacre fled to Geneva for protection. Melville's experience with the evil that kings can do to the church and her members made him a fierce defender of the rights of the church when he returned to Scotland.

Scotland's King James believed that he ruled by divine right. He hated the presbyterian government of the Church of Scotland because he had no control over it. The male members of each Scottish congregation elected the elders and ministers to rule the church. The elders and ministers from the churches in a particular area formed a church court called a presbytery, and once a year elders and ministers from across the nation met for a General Assembly to make decisions for the whole church.

King James wanted the Church of Scotland to be ruled like the Church of England. The Church of England declared that the king was the supreme governor of the church and bishops ruled, not elders and ministers chosen by the people. James insisted that the Church of Scotland should not meet in General Assembly without his permission and that he had the right to overrule any of their decisions. He tried time and again to install bishops to rule the church. Andrew Melville resisted him every step of the way.

Once, the king's council summoned Melville to Edinburgh and charged him with making treasonous speeches against the king.

Melville protested his innocence and presented sworn statements of witnesses who testified that he was a loyal subject who never made treasonous comments. The council ignored the evidence and did not permit him to face his accusers. When Melville complained of the council's unfair treatment, a nobleman interrupted him and said that he was a law breaker and had no right to complain. So Melville unfastened his small Hebrew Bible which he always kept attached to his belt, dropped it on the table and said, "These are my instructions; show me if I broke them."

The nobleman picked up the Hebrew Bible and seeing that it was in a language that he did not understand, he turned to the king and said, "Sire, he scorns your Majesty and the Council!"

"I do not scorn, my lords;" answered Melville, "but I am earnest and zealous for the cause of Christ and His Church."

The council sentenced him to prison. But before they could arrest him, Melville escaped to England. He returned two years later when Presbyterian Scottish nobles forced the king to change his policies and promise to respect the rights of the church. However, King James continued to press his claim that he was the head of the church. The struggle raged back and forth for many years as Melville and his friends fought for a church free from interference from the king.

In 1592, it looked as if the Presbyterians had won. In that year, presbyterian church government was established in Scotland by an act of Parliament which King James reluctantly accepted. This act called for the General Assembly to be held once every year and denied the king the power to appoint bishops. Melville rejoiced that the Church of Scotland could be guided by the Word of God alone and not the dictates of a king.

But King James had no intention of allowing the Church of Scotland to act independently of his wishes. He gradually chipped away at the independence of the church, always with the goal of abolishing Presbyterianism and installing bishops who would follow his directions.

In 1596, the General Assembly of the Church of Scotland had had enough of the king's meddling in church affairs. They dispatched a commission, which included Andrew Melville, to lay their grievances before the king. But scarcely had the men begun to explain their concerns when the king stormed around the room saying that they were the cause of the problem. Then Andrew Melville, unable to bear it any longer, grabbed the king by his sleeve and called him, "God's silly vassal."

"Sir," Melville said, "we will always honor you in public; but since we have this opportunity to speak to your Majesty in private and since the steps you are taking are likely to bring ruin both to you and the country and the Church of God, we must be faithful to God to discharge our duty by telling you the truth. If we do not, we would be traitors both to Christ and to you."

"There are two kings and two kingdoms in Scotland," Melville told him. "There is King James, the head of the commonwealth; and there is Christ Jesus the king of the Church. In Christ's kingdom you are not a king nor a lord nor a head, but a member."

When Melville had finished speaking, the king promised to satisfy their concerns. But King James kept plotting to destroy the Presbyterians.

In 1600, the Presbytery of St. Andrews sent Melville as their representative to the General Assembly. No sooner had he arrived than the king ordered Melville to appear before him immediately. "Why must you be so much trouble?" the king asked.

"My presbytery sent me to represent them here at the General Assembly," he answered. "I dare not disobey for I do not want to displease my Lord who is far higher and greater than any earthly king."

James blurted out his displeasure and ordered Melville to get out. But as Melville left, he held his hand to his throat and said, "Sire, if it is this you want, you shall have it before I betray the cause of Christ!"

When England's Queen Elizabeth died in 1603, King James VI of Scotland was crowned King James I of England. He now reigned over both kingdoms. Before he set off to rule in London, he made a speech in St. Giles Kirk in Edinburgh, declaring to the leaders of the Church of Scotland that he would not try to control them. Not long after he established his reign in England, King James summoned Melville to his court in London.

When Melville arrived in London, officers seized him and brought him to the king's council at Whitehall. The council accused him of treason. They ordered him to apologize and retract what he had written and spoken. But Melville defended his teachings and bluntly pointed out the double dealing of the king and his court. The council stripped him of his position at the University of St. Andrews and cast him into a cell in the Tower of London. Forbidden visitors and pen and paper, he scratched Bible verses on the stone walls with his shoe buckle. Later, when he was allowed writing materials, he wrote a paraphrase of the Psalms in Latin.

In 1611, a French nobleman asked King James to release Melville and permit him to come to France to teach theology at the University of Sedan. After four years imprisonment in the Tower, Melville was banished to France and barred from ever returning to Britain.

While away in France, he often wrote letters to ministers in Scotland, giving them advice and encouragement as they struggled to protect the church from the king's interference. Melville never saw Scotland again. He died in 1622 at the age of seventy-seven.

6

LAURENCE CHADERTON

Master of Emmanuel College

(c. 1537–1640)

On January 16, 1604, Laurence Chaderton and three other Puritan scholars stood with bowed heads in a drawing room of the royal palace at Hampton Court. They were meeting the newly-crowned King James for the first time. They, and nearly 1,000 other ministers of the Church of England, had petitioned James to allow reforms of the church. So James called a conference of church leaders to discuss with him the state of the English church.

The Puritans were greatly outnumbered at the conference. The king had summoned just four of them, but had invited fifty ministers of the episcopal party led by Richard Bancroft, the Bishop of London, who wanted the church to remain as it was. Chaderton and Bancroft were old friends from their college days at Cambridge. Once, in a street fight, Chaderton suffered a serious wound to his hand protecting Bancroft from an angry townsman. But they were on opposite sides now.

The Puritans hoped that since James had been King of Scotland for many years before he also was crowned King of England and had worshipped in the Presbyterian Church of Scotland that he would be sympathetic to their views.

King James sat silently as the Puritans began their appeal, request-ing that church beliefs and practices be made more faithful to the Bible. At this, Bishop Bancroft pled with the king to silence them. "It is not lawful," Bancroft said, "to hear these schismatics criticize their bishops."

But the king told the Puritans to proceed. They asked that godly, well-trained pastors be placed in all the churches to proclaim the good news of Jesus Christ. They called for a new translation of the English Bible to more accurately reflect the original Hebrew and Greek texts. Lastly, they recommended that the bishop in each di-ocese meet with a presbytery of ministers to discuss reforms and implement changes.

At the mention of the word presbytery, King James's cheeks flushed red. He leaned forward in his chair and shot back, "If you aim at a Scottish presbytery, it agrees as well with monarchy as God and the devil."

Raising his voice, he added, "No bishop, no king!"

Then James fixed his gaze on the four Puritans and said, "If this is all your party has to say, I will make them conform, or else I will harass them out of the land, or else do worse."

The stunned Puritans left the conference knowing that the king would never work with them to reform the Church of England. How-ever, James agreed with their request for a new translation of the English Bible. The king called for the best Hebrew and Greek schol-ars in the land to work on it. Laurence Chaderton was one of the first selected to serve on the translation team.

Years earlier, when Chaderton was a student at Christ's College in Cambridge, he was the least likely person to become a prominent minister and defender of biblical Christianity because he had no in-terest in Jesus Christ. Being raised on a well-to-do country estate, he loved the outdoors and spent his time hunting, horseback riding and hawking. At college, his great interests were tennis and archery. His muscular physique came in handy in the frequent fights that broke out between rowdy students and irritated townspeople.

But in the early 1560s when Chaderton entered college, the strug-gle between Roman Catholicism and Protestantism continued to pervade the kingdom. Queen Mary, who had persecuted the Protes-tant reformers and sent hundreds to be burned at the stake, had only been dead for a few years. Her half-sister Elizabeth became queen in her place, and Elizabeth restored the Protestant Reformation in England. Laurence was raised Roman Catholic, and his father was a staunch supporter of the Roman faith.

At Cambridge, students debated the doctrines and practices of the Roman Catholic Church and the Protestant Church of England. Chaderton began to read the arguments for and against the Reformation. For the first time in his life, he carefully searched the Bible to understand its teaching, and he talked with his fellow students about it. After much thought and prayer, Chaderton came to believe that Reformation doctrines were true to the teaching of the Bible. When he expressed his change of mind to his father, his father dismissed it. "Your new opinions are due to the influence of the college," he said.

He told his son that he wanted him to leave the university at once and proceed to the Inns of Court in London to study law. He promised to pay his expenses and grant him a generous allowance if he would do so. Laurence did not wish to alienate his father, but his spiritual convictions were growing deeper. So he wrote him a letter politely declining the offer. Soon afterwards, he received a short note from his father:

"Dear Laurence,

If you will renounce the new sect which you have joined you may expect all the happiness which the care of an indulgent father can secure you. Otherwise, I enclose in this letter a shilling to buy a wallet with. Go and beg for your living. Farewell!"

The loss of his father's support was a great blow, but he pressed on. He took a part-time teaching job, earned a partial scholarship and borrowed money to pay the rest of his college expenses. Laurence changed his major to study theology and to prepare to be a minister. And a few years later, he was ordained a minister in the Church of England.

Instead of taking a call to a parish church, Laurence Chaderton remained at Christ's College where he fulfilled various posts. Being in debt troubled him greatly, and he worked hard to pay off his student loans quickly. Afterwards, he used money frugally, avoided debt and urged his students to do likewise. As a university officer, he continued to study theology, church history, Latin, Greek, and Hebrew. He honed his skills in modern languages becoming fluent in

French, Spanish, and Italian. Although his academic achievements were impressive, it was his preaching that brought him renown.

Students packed the college chapel whenever he preached. Every Sunday, he preached at St. Clement's Church in Cambridge and visited prisoners in Cambridge Castle and preached to them. "He had a wonderful zeal for winning souls," a parishioner said of him.

Many people commented on the effect that Chaderton's prayers had on those who heard them. "His prayers," one observer wrote, "seem to fire the souls of his hearers and carry them with him to heaven."

In 1585, when Sir Walter Mildmay, a wealthy and influential Puritan, wanted to found a college at Cambridge for the purpose of training men to preach the good news of Jesus Christ, he asked Chaderton to lead it. At the same time, Chaderton was offered an important church office which would pay him ten times more than being master of a newly-established college. His friends urged him to accept the more prestigious and lucrative position. When he told Mildmay that he was considering taking the church office, Mildmay replied, "If you won't be master, I certainly am not going to found the college."

So Chaderton took the job of master of Emmanuel College. He threw himself into the hard work of creating a college from scratch. "I have planted an acorn," Mildmay told Queen Elizabeth when the college began, "and when it becomes an oak, only God knows what it will amount to."

Chaderton guided Emmanuel with wisdom and energy. It quickly grew and produced a great number of learned and godly men who embraced Chaderton's Puritan convictions. They became great preachers and reformers in the English Church. Emmanuel College not only became the center for Puritan influence in Britain, but also left its mark on New England—producing notable ministers and leaders in the colonies such as John Cotton and John Harvard, the founder of Harvard College in Cambridge, Massachusetts.

Laurence Chaderton also preached when he visited other parts of the kingdom. Once in his travels, he had heard about a church in a town near Manchester where the people rarely went to church. Chaderton decided to fill the pulpit there for several weeks. Soon, ten times as many people came to worship as had before. Once, after preaching a long sermon for two hours, he said, "I have tired your patience and I will close now."

But the whole congregation urged him to continue. "For God's sake, sir," a man shouted, "go on, we beg you, go on!"

And so he extended his sermon for another hour to the great delight and blessing of the people.

When King James authorized a new translation of the Bible, Chaderton served on a committee that translated several Old Testament books, including Psalms and Proverbs. After a few years of work, the Authorized Version of the English Bible—often called the King James Version—was published.

When he was 87 years old—after leading Emmanuel College for nearly forty years—Chaderton decided to resign as master. He gathered the faculty to inform them. "I cannot, owing to my age, do my duty," he said. "Some things I have not attended to as they should be, for which I crave God's pardon."

With his eyes swollen with tears, he told them he needed to resign, "It is for the good of the college," he said.

As he spoke, one professor interrupted him, saying, "We beseech you not to do it."

"Do not hinder me," Chaderton answered, "I am doing it in the name of the Lord."

As he bid them farewell and handed the keys of the college to the senior fellow, all broke down in tears.

After his resignation one nobleman offered to win him a bishopric in the church, but he rejected the offer. "I am content with my lot," he said.

He remained in Cambridge and rejoiced to see the college thrive under his successors. Chaderton lived to be 103 years old—his mind and memory remained strong until the end. One man who knew him well said, "He lived to free men's souls from the slavery of ignorance and sin and win them to Christ."

7

JOHN ROBINSON

Pastor to the Pilgrim Fathers

(1575–1625)

In the fall of 1604, King James I who had recently come to the throne of England tightened the screws on the Puritans. Convinced that the security of his reign rested on his control of the church, James ordered his bishops to demand full conformity in every parish to the Church of England's prayer book for worship. When John Robinson refused to use some of the ceremonies required by the prayer book that he considered unbiblical, a church court expelled him from his church and threw him out of his house. "I might have enjoyed my liberty and peace," Robinson said, "if I were willing to conform."

Being deprived of his living and home drove Robinson to reexamine his views. He went back to Cambridge where he had earned his degree to consult with some of the university's Puritan theologians. He pored over the Scriptures and read books on theology and church government to be certain of what he believed.

"Was the Church of England a true church ordered by the Scriptures?" Robinson asked himself. "Was the rule of bishops God's will for the church? Could the Church of England, the official state church, ever be reformed according to the Bible?"

After careful study of the New Testament's teaching about church government, Robinson came to believe that the Church of England was not organized according to the Word of God. He now thought that when a local body of Christians united to worship together, they formed a true church and could choose and ordain their officers. Robinson had become a Congregationalist. Congregationalists were also called Separatists or Independents because they had separated from the Church of England.

He found an independent congregation in Scrooby, a village in the Midlands, and began to worship with them. They met for worship in Scrooby Manor, the country home of William Brewster, one of the leading members of the congregation. But these were difficult days for anyone separating from the state church. It was against the law not to attend a parish church. Ministers who preached without the permission of the bishop faced imprisonment and the confiscation of their property. When constables began to raid Separatists' meetings and levied fines on the congregants, the Scrooby congregation met secretly in different locations to avoid detection and arrest. Although they were unwelcome in England, it was against the law to leave England without the king's permission.

After several years of threats, fines, and imprisonment, the Scrooby Separatists decided to flee to Holland. The Dutch permitted religious liberty in their land and hundreds of English Puritans and Separatists had already started new lives there. In the fall of 1607, the leaders of the Scrooby congregation paid an English sea captain to secretly transport them. At the arranged time, the captain brought them onboard his ship, but he had betrayed them. Moments later, government officials came and arrested them, stealing their valuables as they carted them off to jail. After several weeks of imprisonment, they were released.

A few months later, the Scrooby believers arranged with a Dutch captain to pick them up on the banks of the Humber River near Hull and bring them to Amsterdam. One of the small landing boats ran aground before the Dutch ship could load everyone. Then constables arrived and arrested many who remained onshore. Those already onboard sailed to Holland. The leaders of the congregation realized that fleeing in a large group was too dangerous. So over the course of several months, they slipped the remaining members out of the country in small groups.

Not long after arriving in Amsterdam, the congregation moved to Leiden. They chose John Robinson as their pastor and William Brewster their ruling elder. Robinson bought a house in the city with a big room where they held their worship services.

He preached the good news of Jesus Christ, making it clear that sinners were saved only by the grace of God through Christ's sacrifice on the cross. Robinson also taught that true faith must shine forth in obedience and love. "God does not regard church and chamber religion towards Him," he said, "which is not accompanied in the house and streets with loving kindness and mercy and all goodness towards men."

During the week, they gathered for Bible study and prayer. Robinson, a cheerful man, visited from house to house, encouraging his people in the truth, instructing the children and comforting the sick. One of the members of the congregation, William Bradford, said, "We enjoyed much sweet and delightful fellowship and spiritual comfort together in the ways of God under the able ministry and prudent government of Mr. John Robinson and Mr. William Brewster. We lived together in peace and love and holiness."

Many in England criticized them for abandoning their homeland. In their defense, Robinson wrote, "We do not forsake our country, but are by it forsaken and expelled by most extreme laws and violent prescriptions."

Although forsaken by men, Robinson and his flock did not feel forsaken by God. "Although we are constrained to live in a foreign land," Robinson prayed, "exiled from country, spoiled of goods, destitute of friends, few in number, and lowly in condition, yet we are, for all that, not less acceptable to You, our gracious God."

In England, church officials tightly controlled the printing of books. Every book had to be licensed by a bishop. Consequently, it was nearly impossible for books supporting congregational church government to be published in the kingdom. But in Holland, books of all sorts could be printed. Robinson began to write.

William Brewster purchased a printing press and started publishing Robinson's books and pamphlets. In 1610, Robinson's book, *Justification of Separation*, which defended the right of Christians to form independent congregations, began to be smuggled into England.

When Robinson's books made their way across England, they came to the attention of King James. James resented Robinson's teachings against the king as the head of the church. He regarded John Robinson and William Brewster enemies of the state.

Meanwhile, the church in Leiden continued to grow. As Englishmen fled from religious persecution in their homeland to Holland, some made their way to Leiden. After hearing Robinson preach and seeing the Christian character of his people, many joined the congregation.

At that time, a great controversy between Calvinists and Arminians arose in Leiden. It involved the great question of predestination and free will. Did man play a part in his salvation by choosing God, or was salvation completely a gift of God's free grace? Throughout Holland and especially in the city of Leiden, merchants and peasants, the learned and the laborer, debated the roles of man's free will and God's sovereign rule. John Robinson entered the fray on the side of those who believed that God chose his people and poured out His Spirit into their hearts that they might believe. He debated with the theologians at Leiden University, and he wrote books exalting God's sovereign power in salvation.

Life in Holland was hard for the exiles. They missed their homeland, and they were concerned for their children. They wanted a quality Christian education for their children in English. Some of their sons joined the Dutch army or became sailors on Dutch trading ships and drifted away from the church.

So the Scrooby exiles in Leiden made plans to move to North America. In 1607, the Virginia Company in London had planted a colony at Jamestown, Virginia. The King of England was anxious to establish colonies in the New World to strengthen English land claims and expand trade.

The Scrooby exiles petitioned the English government for permission to start a settlement in America. King James was willing to permit them to go to the New World, but he would not grant them religious liberty. However, he said he would leave them alone if they lived peacefully there.

When word reached Leiden that the king would not grant them the right to worship God as they liked in North America, discouragement fell over the church. They feared that they would sell their

JOHN ROBINSON

"The travelers saw Pastor Robinson fall on his knees in prayer with tears streaming down his cheeks."

possessions and risk all to sail to the shores of the New World only to be persecuted again by the Crown. But Robinson was more optimistic. He told his flock that even if the king had granted permission, he could change his mind at any time. He challenged them to trust themselves to God's care as they had always done before.

After a day of fasting and prayer, the congregation voted to uproot themselves again and start anew in the wilderness of North America. They agreed that the youngest and the strongest should go first. The stronger members could build cabins and plant crops, making it easier for the rest of the church to follow later. They decided that Pastor Robinson should remain in Leiden and come over in a year or two with the others. After several months of planning, they hired a ship called the Mayflower to take them across the Atlantic.

Before they left Leiden, the congregation met at Robinson's house. He preached a sermon about trusting God and serving Him in difficult circumstances. "We are soon to part and the Lord knows whether we should live to see one another again," he said. "If God should reveal anything to you by any other instrument of His, be ready to receive it as ever you were to receive any truth by my ministry. I am confident that the Lord has more truth and light yet to break forth out of His holy Word."

Robinson and the members that remained in Leiden walked to the harbor to see their friends off. It was a warm July day when they set sail for England and then the New World. As the ship pulled away from its moorings, the travelers saw Pastor Robinson fall on his knees in prayer with tears streaming down his cheeks. "Truly doleful was the sight of that sad and mournful parting," one remembered, "to see what sighs and sobs and prayers did sound among them, what tears did gush from every eye; that even the Dutch strangers who stood on the dock as spectators could not keep from tears."

Pastor Robinson gave a letter to his departing friends to read on the Mayflower as they crossed the Atlantic Ocean. "Loving Christian friends," he wrote, "I do heartily salute you all in the Lord with whom I am present in my best affection and most earnest longings after you. I am constrained for a while to be bodily absent from you. God knows how willingly I would have been with you were I not by strong necessity held back for the present."

Little did any of them realize the difficulties and trials that awaited the brothers and sisters who sailed to America. They had planned to arrive in late summer when they could build shelters and plant crops before winter. But delays and fierce Atlantic storms slowed the journey. The howling winds and driving rains of a fast-approaching winter greeted the Mayflower when it finally arrived in the New World in November of 1620. They landed at Plymouth Rock in present-day Massachusetts—not in Virginia, and hastily built some primitive shelters. Soon sickness overwhelmed them. In the first two months of 1621, one or two of the benighted settlers died every day. At times, only a few had the strength to bring food and water to the sick and dying. By the end of winter, half of the Leiden pilgrims were dead and buried.

In June 1621, when Robinson received word that nearly fifty members of his flock had died at Plymouth, he wrote the survivors: "My continual prayers are to the Lord for you; my utmost earnest desire is to be with you... The deaths of so many, our dear friends and brethren, Oh! How grievous... But God has tempered judgment with mercy in sparing the rest. God, I hope, has given you the victory after many difficulties."

During this same time, Robinson and his wife lost two of their children to a plague that swept through Leiden. He learned to lean on God in the midst of trials. "The Lord provides very graciously for His poor servants in distress," he wrote, "as they have very little else save the promises of God by which to comfort themselves."

Robinson did everything in his power to join his flock in Plymouth, but the authorities in London did not permit it. They did not want Robinson, the great champion of congregationalism, in the New World.

In November 1621 and again in the summer of 1623, when ships arrived at Plymouth carrying more of their friends from Leiden, the hearts of the settlers sank to find that their beloved Pastor Robinson was not among them. The settlers languished without their minister. One wrote, "The more is our grief that our pastor is kept from us, by whom we might enjoy the Lord's Supper every Sabbath and baptisms as often as there were occasions of children to baptize."

"My heart is with you," Robinson wrote them. "May God bring us together, if it be His will, and keep us faithful to the end."

Although Robinson desperately wanted to be with his people in America, he accepted the fact that God ruled over all circumstances. "If this or that good thing be indeed for my good," he wrote, "I shall receive it from Him in due time. And if I receive it not, it is a real testimony from Him that indeed it is not good for me, no matter how much I desire it."

Robinson closely followed the trials and triumphs of his friends in Plymouth—praying for them constantly and offering encouragement and counsel by letter. When he received word that the settlers had killed seven Indians who had conspired to attack them, he grieved the loss of life and questioned the brutality of it. He wrote a letter to William Bradford who had been elected governor of Plymouth colony. "Concerning the killing of those poor Indians," Robinson wrote, "how happy a thing it would have been if you had converted some, before you had killed any. Besides, where blood once begins to be shed, it is seldom staunched for a long time after."

In 1625, John Robinson fell sick. In a matter of a few days, he died. One heartbroken member of the Leiden church wrote to Bradford at Plymouth: "It has pleased the Lord to take out of this vale of tears your and our loving and faithful pastor, Mr. John Robinson. He, having safely finished his course and performed his work which the Lord had appointed him here to perform, now rests with the Lord in eternal happiness."

Robinson's death was a great blow to the Plymouth settlers. "The news struck them with sorrow and sadness," William Bradford wrote. "It is a marvel that it did not wholly discourage them and sink them."

John Robinson's influence lived on for many years. During the dark days of Charles I and the English Civil War, many read Robinson's writings on Congregationalism. His books and the godly examples of his churches in Leiden and Plymouth helped to make congregational church government popular in America and England.

William Bradford beautifully summarized the influence that Robinson had on his congregation: "Such was the mutual love and respect that this worthy man had to his flock, and his flock to him, that it was hard to judge whether he delighted more in having such a people, or they in having such a pastor. Though they esteemed him highly while he labored among them, yet much more after his death when they came to feel the want of his help and saw what a treasure they had lost."

8

RICHARD ROGERS AND JOHN ROGERS

Prince of Preachers

(1551–1618 and 1572–1636)

In the 1560s, an Englishman coined the name "Puritan," a term meant to mock Christians who took their faith seriously and sought to walk in careful obedience to the commandments of God. To those who did not guide their consciences by the Bible, the Puritans were overly scrupulous spoilsports.

One day, Richard Rogers, the minister at Wethersfield, Essex, spent the afternoon with the local lord of the manor. Although Rogers had a reputation of being a cheerful, kind-hearted, and generous man, he kept a close watch on his speech and behavior, striving to avoid sin. "Mr. Rogers," the nobleman said to him, "I like you and your company very well, only you are too precise."

"Oh sir," replied Rogers, "I serve a precise God."

Richard Rogers strove to keep his eyes fixed on heaven. "I should be very sorry," he often said, "if I did not employ every day as if it were my last."

He kept a spiritual diary to examine his fellowship with Christ and his obedience to Christ's commands—a practice that other Puritans would follow. His love for Christ, his tender conscience and his kindness impressed all who knew him. One churchman looking back on Rogers's life remarked, "England hardly ever brought forth a man who walked more closely with God."

Through his forthright preaching, he led many to a living faith in Jesus Christ. "The Lord honored none more in the conversion of souls," a fellow minister said of him.

However, church officials who wanted to suppress the influence of the Puritans often disrupted Rogers's work. In 1583, when the Archbishop of Canterbury, John Whitgift, insisted on strict conformity to all the standards and practices of the church, Rogers lead twenty-six ministers to petition Queen Elizabeth for relief. Archbishop Whitgift summarily suspended them from office and banned them from preaching until they conformed to every jot and tittle of his demands.

After eight months, an influential nobleman intervened on Rogers's behalf, and got him reinstated to his pulpit. Over the next three decades, Richard Rogers faced periodic harassment and trouble from the archbishop for his unwillingness to conform to all the dictates of the prelates of the Church of England.

In 1603, when Rogers and six other ministers refused to take an oath promising to provide testimony against themselves, Whitgift suspended them from preaching. He ordered them to appear before him at the Court of High Commission, but the day they were to appear at the court, Archbishop Whitgift died, and the charges were dropped.

However, the new Archbishop of Canterbury, Richard Bancroft, despised the Puritans as much as his predecessor. At times, he banned Rogers from preaching, making his flock languish without his ministry. "It greatly troubles me," Rogers said, "that after laboring between thirty and forty years in the ministry, I am accounted unworthy to preach, while so many idle and scandalous persons enjoy their ease and liberty."

Bancroft repeatedly cited Rogers for his unwillingness to conform to every practice of the church, forcing him to make long and costly journeys to the archbishop's court. At the same time, the Bishop of London also hounded Rogers and his fellow Puritans. Summoning Rogers to appear before him in London, the bishop told him, "By the help of Jesus, I will not leave one preacher in my diocese that does not conform."

But the bishop died before he could act on his threats. "I was much in prayer about my troubles," Rogers wrote in his diary, "God has to my own comfort, and the comfort of my people, delivered me once more out of my troubles. Oh, that I may make a holy use of my liberty."

Like many other Puritans, Rogers had a high regard for education. He believed that the health of the church depended on well-educated and equipped pastors. So he started a school in his home to prepare young men for university and to encourage them to become ministers.

He took a particular interest in a close relative of his named John Rogers. Seeing that John had a bright mind but no money to pay for college, Richard Rogers paid for his books and helped to support him at the University of Cambridge. But John, a foolish young man addicted to vice, soon sold his books and spent the money on his sinful pleasures. Despite the irresponsibility and ingratitude of his relative, Richard sought out John, pointed out the error of his ways and convinced him to try again. Richard bought him a fresh supply of books, and sent him back to Cambridge. But John quickly fell back into his old habits. He had sold his books again, left the university and squandered the money as before.

After learning that John had wasted his generosity and the opportunity of a university education for a second time, Richard Rogers decided to give up on the young man. But his wife urged him not to abandon John to his folly. "Give him one more chance," she told her husband. Against his better judgment, Richard Rogers paid for John's college tuition and books and sent him back to Cambridge for a third time. While there, the Spirit of God made John a new man. He excelled in his studies and became widely known for his devotion to Christ. Before long, he was preaching the good news of Christ as a minister in Dedham, a town not far from Wethersfield. John and Richard Rogers met often with other like-minded ministers for prayer and mutual encouragement.

John Rogers preached with conviction and energy—arresting the attention of his hearers and forcefully applying biblical truths to their lives. People long remembered his animated and heart-piercing sermons. "His words were as sparks of fire," one observer said.

When John preached on Sundays and on Tuesday mornings, large crowds filled the spacious sanctuary that seated 1,200 people. Those who arrived late were turned away for lack of room. In good weather, he preached from the outside porch of the church where several thousand people could hear him. By God's grace, he shook careless sinners out of their spiritual slumber. Many people put their trust in Christ through his preaching. One Puritan minister called John Rogers "one of the most awakening preachers of the age."

Seeing how powerfully the Lord blessed his relative's ministry, Richard Rogers used to say, "I will never despair of any man, for John Rogers's sake."

It was not unusual for students to ride on horseback the forty miles from Cambridge to hear him. One Cambridge scholar who made the journey was Thomas Goodwin. Goodwin would later become one of the most influential Puritans in the kingdom. On the day of Goodwin's visit, John Rogers preached on the inspiration of Scripture. He told the congregation that in their Bibles they possessed the very Word of God, and yet they neglected to read it and apply it. "The Lord is saying to you," Rogers said, "Well, I have trusted you so long with my Bible, but you have slighted it. It lies in your houses, covered with dust and cobwebs, but you care not to look at it. Do you use my Bible so? Well, you shall have my Bible no longer!"

Rogers lifted up his Bible from the pulpit and began to carry it away. But then he turned around, fell to his knees, and spoke on behalf of the people to God. "Lord," he cried out, "whatever you do to us, take not your Bible from us. Burn our houses, destroy our goods, only spare us our Bible!"

Then Rogers rose to his feet and impersonated the words of God again. "Say you so? Well, I will try you a little longer."

Rogers stretched out his hands, held the Bible toward the people and said, "Here is my Bible for you. I will see how you will use it, whether you will love it more and live more according to it!"

Reflecting on their neglect of the Scriptures, many broke down in tears. Thomas Goodwin wept for some time in the pew after the service. Finally, he got up and walked outside and prepared to return to the university. But overcome with remorse again, he hung on the neck of his horse, weeping for a quarter of an hour, before he regained the strength to mount up and ride home. Goodwin never forgot the sermon, and he often thanked God for its message.

Goodwin was not the only minister who, in their youth, found great blessing through Rogers's preaching. Giles Firmin, a Puritan preacher and writer, traced his conversion to a visit he made to Rogers's church when he was just a school boy. On that day, a crowd pressed to enter the overflowing church. As Firmin and some of his playmates strained to slip in, they caught the eye of John Rogers. "Here are some young ones come for Christ," Rogers cried out, motioning to the crowd to make room for the boys. Then looking at Firmin and his friends, he said, "Will nothing satisfy you until you have Christ? Then you shall have Him."

Then Rogers preached a sermon on forgiveness in Jesus Christ. After the message, Giles Firmin believed in Christ as his Savior and followed Him for the rest of his life.

As the persecution against Puritans increased, some decided to move to the wilderness of North America and plant a colony where they would be free to worship God as they saw fit. John Rogers's preaching was greatly admired by those who decided to escape to the New World, and Rogers encouraged them in their plans. In 1630, some people from Rogers's congregation were among those who sailed to Massachusetts.

Before they set sail, Rogers got word that they were in great need. Rogers sent money and a letter to Governor Winthrop. "This day," he wrote, "I have received so lamentable a letter from John Page who has his wife and two children there, and he informs me that unless God stirs up some friends to send him some provision, he is likely to starve. Now I pity the man much and have sent you twenty shillings, entreating you, for God's sake, to provide such a barrel of meal as this money will buy, and give it to John Page . . . It cuts me to the heart to hear that any of our neighbors should be like to famish . . . I commend you and the weighty business you are about to the blessing of Almighty God."

Despite the vast numbers who learned the Word of God from John Rogers and the countless people that he led to Christ, church authorities moved to suppress him. In 1626, William Laud, the Bishop of London, tried to force all the ministers to conform to his requirements for worship. When Rogers refused to submit to the unbiblical practices, Bishop Laud banned him from preaching and withheld his salary. The ban broke Rogers's heart and put a great financial strain on his large family. "Let them take me and hang me up by the neck," he said, "if they will but remove those stumbling blocks out of the church."

After a year, Rogers accepted the bishop's requirements, and he was reinstated as a preacher. Soon, his conscience bothered him for having agreed to conform. So he took a stand to omit the unbiblical demands of the bishop. "If I come into trouble for nonconformity," he said, "I resolve by God's assistance to come away with a clear conscience. For though the liberty of my ministry is dear to me, I dare not buy it at such a rate. If I am urged again I never will yield. It was my weakness before which I beseech God to pardon."

However, when the bishop removed John Rogers from his ministry a second time for nonconformity, he again agreed to conform. This failure of nerve cast him into despair and he soon repented of it, whereupon he was banned from his ministry for good.

Long after his death in 1636, he was fondly remembered and highly regarded by believers in England and America. The famous minister of Connecticut, Thomas Hooker, who knew Rogers before Hooker immigrated to the New World, always called John Rogers "the prince of all the preachers of England."

9

RICHARD SIBBES

Heaven Was In Him, Before He Was In Heaven

(1577–1635)

One Sunday in January of 1630, Bishop of London, William Laud, presided over a worship service to consecrate a new church in the heart of London. Laud orchestrated every detail—beginning with the bishop and his entourage of clerics, dressed in robes and surplices of brilliant colors, processing around the outside of the church. When they approached the west door, a chorus of voices cried out on cue, "Open, open, ye everlasting doors that the King of glory may enter in!"

At that, the doors flung open and Bishop Laud marched in. He fell to his knees, lifted his face toward heaven, spread out his arms and said, "This place is holy. The ground is holy. In the name of the Father, Son, and Holy Ghost, I pronounce it holy."

The worship service—filled with bowing to the east, sprinkling dust and chanting prayers—proceeded with much pomp until the train of churchmen paraded out.

Not far away at Gray's Inn, a church in central London, a very different kind of worship service was in progress. Richard Sibbes, dressed in a plain black robe, preached a clear sermon that all in the congregation—noblemen and commoners, university educated and illiterate—could understand. "Come boldly to the throne of grace," he preached. "Be of good comfort, God calls you. Never fear to go to God since we have such a Mediator with Him that is not only our friend, but our brother and husband."

Sunday by Sunday for the last fourteen years, Sibbes had preached the Word of God to his flock, seeking to win them to Christ. He had a tender heart for the man or woman weighed down by fears and sins—the "bruised reed" he called them. In nearly all his sermons he included a word of encouragement for them. "Shall our sins discourage us?" he asked his hearers. "No sin is so great but Christ and His mercies are greater," he answered. "The victory lies not upon us, but upon Christ."

"God delights to show his strength in weakness," he assured the fainthearted.

Sibbes—like his fellow Puritans—taught that everything a follower of Christ does should be done to the glory of God with thanksgiving. "The whole life of a Christian should be nothing but praises and thanks to God," he preached. "We should neither eat nor sleep, but eat to God and sleep to God and work to God and talk to God, do all to His glory and praise."

His congregation grew rapidly and overfilled the large sanctuary, so the church wardens built galleries along the walls to accommodate the crowds that came to hear him. And his preaching bore fruit. "No man ever got so far into my heart," a parishioner said.

"He was a worthy instrument of bringing many sons and daughters unto God," one man recorded, "and edifying and building up others."

Sibbes preached at Gray's Inn on Sundays, but during the week he led St. Catharine's College in Cambridge, training young men for the ministry. Under Sibbes's teaching and preaching, an awakening of faith in Christ broke out among the university students.

Although Richard Sibbes was a loyal churchman, happy to use the Book of Common Prayer in worship, he mourned the movement led by Bishop Laud that preferred rituals over sound gospel preaching. Laud called his approach to worship "The beauty of holiness." Sibbes called it "vainglory." "They, out of the pride of their heart, carry themselves very unkindly toward Christ," Sibbes wrote about Laud and his followers. "They are ashamed of the simplicity of the gospel and count preaching foolishness."

Laud won the favor of King Charles I by supporting his claim that he possessed absolute power from God to rule. In court sermons, Laud preached that subjects must submit to the king in all things—to question the king was to question God. He taught that Parliament existed only to do the king's bidding. Any efforts to limit the king's power were treasonous. Charles I and William Laud shared a common hatred for Puritans, and they strove together to root out nonconformity from the kingdom.

When King Charles made Laud Archbishop of Canterbury—the chief prelate of the land—Laud used his position to remake the Church of England after his own image. He was determined to force high-church episcopal worship and doctrine on every congregation. Laud despised the biblical doctrine that proclaims that sinners come to Christ as a gift of God's free grace. He wanted his clergy to emphasize man's good works over the grace of God in salvation. When a parish needed a new minister, Laud placed a man there who embraced his beliefs and practices. Laud's bishops kept young Puritan preachers from serving in churches. Ministers who resisted the new ceremonies were ejected from their pulpits and Laud replaced them with his men.

Richard Sibbes knew the English people were starving for spiritual food, while the churchmen gave them ceremonies empty of the good news of Christ. "The children cry for the bread of life," he wrote, "and there is none to give them." He had long desired to have the young men that he and other Puritans trained for the ministry at Cambridge preaching in every part of the country. "If we could set up some lights in all the dark corners of this kingdom," he said, "that might shine to those people that sit in darkness and in the shadow of death."

At that time, the local nobleman in many churches had the right to appoint the minister of the parish. This right called patronage could be purchased, if the nobleman was willing to sell it. Sibbes and a dozen other leading Puritans—including several wealthy noblemen—hatched a plan to raise funds to buy patronage rights in churches and place faithful preachers in the pulpits.

For seven years, they worked behind the scenes, planting Puritan preachers in churches across the kingdom. But then Laud convinced the courts to stop the purchases of patronage rights. "They are the main instruments for the Puritan faction to undo the church," Laud said.

Roused to anger by Sibbes's preaching and his efforts to install Puritan ministers, Laud summoned Sibbes and a few other leading Puritan ministers to stand trial before the Star Chamber, the king's secret court. "We now face a fierce storm from the enraged spirits of the bishops," Sibbes wrote to a friend. "I expect soon to be deprived of my pastoral charge. But I am in God's hands, not in theirs, to whose good pleasure I do contentedly and cheerfully submit myself."

He did not let trials dampen his faith. "Whatsoever is good for God's children," he said, "they shall have it. Therefore, if poverty be good they shall have it; if disgrace or crosses be good they shall have them."

The commissioners of the Star Chamber found Sibbes and the others guilty. They ordered the men expelled from their pulpits and levied large fines upon them. Some of them fled to the American colonies or Holland. Some of them remained in England to await their fate. Sibbes waited to be expelled from his church and college, but the sentence was never carried out. Most likely, influential friends of Sibbes intervened to prevent it. So Sibbes carried on his preaching and teaching.

Others who crossed Laud were not so fortunate. Alexander Leighton, a minister who wrote against the rule of bishops, was brought before the Star Chamber. Laud demanded the harshest punishment possible. The court condemned Leighton to barbaric torture. They ordered an axeman to publicly whip him, cut off his ears, brand both cheeks with a hot iron, and then cast him into prison for life. When the sentence was read out in court, Laud shouted, "Give thanks to God who has given me the victory over my enemies."

Many details of Sibbes's life are unknown because he rarely talked or wrote about himself. His focus was Jesus Christ. "Let us labor to be good in secret," he preached. "As Christ lived a hidden life—that is, he was not known for who he was so that he might work our salvation—so let us be content to be hidden ones."

The only reason his sermons and writings were published was because his friends insisted on it. His books won praise from readers in Britain and America. He was called "The Sweet Dropper" because his works dropped the sweet fragrance of Christ.

Richard Sibbes worked and preached until the day he passed away. The text for his last sermons came from John chapter 14—Christ's words to his disciples at the Last Supper. "Let not your heart be troubled; believe in God, believe also in me. In my father's house are many mansions; if it were not so, I would've told you."

The day before he died at the age of fifty-eight, he wrote, "I commend my soul into the hands of my gracious Savior who has redeemed it with his most precious blood."

His funeral service was packed with sad but grateful believers from London and Cambridge. A plaque to his memory was installed in a London church. Its first line read: "Servant of God! Well done."

William Laud's end could not have been more different. In 1641, when Parliament began to assert its authority in the land, they called Laud to account for his abuse of power and the persecution of his enemies. He was imprisoned for treason in the Tower of London and then beheaded. Few mourned his passing.

Although Richard Sibbes never married, he left behind many spiritual sons and daughters. Through his preaching at Cambridge, he led John Cotton to faith in Christ. Cotton became the most influential preacher of New England. For the rest of his life, Cotton kept a portrait of Sibbes in his study as a grateful reminder of him.

Sibbes inspired Thomas Goodwin when he was a student at Cambridge to give his life to Christ-centered preaching. "Young man," Sibbes told Goodwin, "if you ever would do good, you must preach the gospel and the free grace of God in Christ Jesus." Goodwin went on to write some of the best works of Christian theology.

Richard Baxter, the famous pastor and theologian, said that reading one of Sibbes's books when he was a boy changed his life. "One day," Baxter wrote, "a poor peddler came to the door. And my father bought from him Dr. Sibbes's *Bruised Reed*. This opened the love of God to me and gave me a livelier understanding of redemption and how much I was beholden to Jesus Christ."

One minister who admired Sibbes's books wrote a two line poem of appreciation.

Of this blest man, let this just praise be given,
Heaven was in him, before he was in heaven.

10

JOHN COTTON

Patriarch of New England

(1584–1652)

In 1609, a throng of black-robed students and professors filed into Great St. Mary's, the stately university church of Cambridge, to hear twenty-five-year-old John Cotton, a fellow of Emmanuel College. Several months earlier, Cotton had preached there to great acclaim. Although his message lacked biblical truth, it brimmed with witty phrases and references to classical authors and rhetorical flourishes which delighted his hearers.

At that time, the university was divided. Some embraced the evangelical faith of the Puritan preachers and professors like Richard Sibbes and the late William Perkins. Others disdained the Puritans' emphasis on repentance and trust in Christ alone for salvation. They preferred a sophisticated religion of ethics and philosophy—not faith in a crucified Savior.

John Cotton had despised the Puritans. He particularly disliked the preaching of William Perkins whose simple gospel sermons awakened his conscience and exposed his pride. The day Perkins died, church bells rang the death knell throughout Cambridge in his honor. When Cotton heard the bells, he rejoiced. "I won't be troubled by him anymore," he said to himself. "He will never again lay siege to my heart."

What the crowd at Great St. Mary's that day did not know was that John Cotton was a changed man. In the months since his last message, Cotton had been wracked by a guilty conscience. His secret rejoicing at the death of Perkins exposed his pettiness and hollow religion. Troubled in heart and mind, he heard Richard Sibbes preach about the hopeless condition of people who trusted in their own righteousness. "Only those who flee to Jesus Christ for the forgiveness of their sins are saved," Sibbes said. As Cotton listened, he saw himself for who he truly was—a helpless sinner in need of a Savior. He put his trust in Christ.

As Cotton stood in the old stone pulpit of Great St. Mary's and began to speak, he abandoned his soaring rhetoric and quotes from philosophers and poets. He preached on Jesus' death on the cross and called everyone in the congregation to give their hearts to Christ. Cotton knew by the scowls on many faces that his sermon was not well received. Instead of enthusiastic congratulations that he had received the last time he had spoken there, the audience left the church with few saying a word to him. He returned to his room downhearted, feeling he had done a poor job in presenting the gospel of his Lord.

But minutes later, John Preston, a fellow of Queen's College, came to his door. Preston told him that he had come to church that day hoping to be entertained by Cotton. "At first I was angry when you began to preach," Preston told him, "but before you finished, I was cut to the heart."

Preston asked him how he could find peace with God. Before he left the room, he believed in Christ for the forgiveness of his sins. Cotton rejoiced that his first evangelical sermon had borne good fruit. John Preston became an influential preacher, and the two men became lifelong friends.

When John Cotton was twenty-eight years old, the officers of St. Boltoph's church in Boston, a city about one hundred miles northeast of London, asked him to preach. Their pastor had left, and they were looking for a new minister. They hoped that Cotton might become their pastor.

The large congregation was divided. Some favored the Puritan message of trusting in Christ for salvation and living a holy life. Others came to church on Sunday mornings and then wanted to live the rest of the time for themselves. The mayor of the town and about half the members of the congregation did not want a Puritan like John Cotton to be their pastor. After the people heard Cotton preach, the mayor brought in another candidate for the church to consider for the job.

When it came time for the congregation to choose a new pastor, the votes were evenly divided between Cotton and the other candidate. It was up to the mayor to cast the deciding vote. But by some error, the mayor marked his ballot for John Cotton. As soon as he realized what he had done, the mayor's cheeks flushed red and he cried out, "Wait! I made a mistake. We need to vote again." So the people voted again. When the ballots were counted, half the votes were for Cotton and half for the other minister. It was up to the mayor to break the tie again. To the surprise of everyone, he mistakenly cast his vote for Cotton a second time.

The flustered mayor insisted that ballots be cast again. But the people refused to vote a third time. "This must be God's will," they said. So Cotton became their pastor.

Despite the strange circumstances of his call, he soon earned the respect of all. Pouring himself into the work, he spent twelve hours each day in study and prayer to prepare the five sermons he preached each week. Cotton preached—sometimes with tears—urging his people to trust completely in Christ. "It was the main bent and aim of Mr. Cotton's ministry," one man said, "to preach a crucified Savior."

Before long, hundreds of people turned from their sins and put their faith in Christ. Fishermen, farmers, and milkmaids began to follow Jesus. "The Spirit of God worked so powerfully through his ministry," one member of his congregation said, "that a great reformation was made in the town." His parishioners filled the great stone church whenever he preached. Even the mayor came to believe in Christ and happily counted himself among the Puritans.

Cotton never made a display of his learning in the pulpit, wanting everyone to comprehend the good news of Jesus Christ. "I desire to speak," he said, "so as to be understood by the most simple."

After hearing Cotton preach, a visiting Dutch scholar said, "Never in my life have I seen such a combination of learning and simplicity as there was in the preaching of that worthy man."

At that time, the leaders of the Church of England placed more importance on ceremonies than on solid sermons based on the Bible. John Cotton and other Puritans thought the church's worship rules about ministers' robes, kneeling for communion, lighting candles and the like were a distraction. The message of Jesus Christ's death on the cross for sinners got lost in all the rituals. So Cotton began to leave out ceremonies from church services that he thought were unbiblical.

But King Charles I and his bishops demanded that all the ministers and people in the land worship God in the ways that they required. They expelled many ministers from their churches who would not conform to all their rituals in worship, and threw some into prison. "They are all church and no Christ," Cotton said about the bishops.

To escape the persecution, some Puritans fled to Holland. One group got the king's permission to start a colony on Massachusetts Bay in North America. They hoped that if they lived far away across the Atlantic Ocean from the king, they could worship God according to the Bible. When a group of Puritans sailed for Massachusetts in 1630 under the leadership of Governor John Winthrop, several members of Cotton's church went with them. In Massachusetts, the colonists built small towns. They named one "Boston" after their hometown in England.

In the meantime, church leaders hauled Cotton before a church court and suspended him from preaching for a time. When the persecution heated up in 1632, officials summoned him to appear before the royal court. He knew that they planned to imprison him.

So Cotton and his wife Sarah fled. For months, they were on the run—hiding from the authorities. After receiving an invitation from Governor Winthrop to come to Massachusetts Bay, Cotton decided to go to America. But escaping out of the kingdom would not be easy. The Crown warned all seaports to be on the lookout for John Cotton, and the king's agents combed the ports to seize him.

In July 1633, Cotton, disguised as a seafarer, and Sarah snuck onto a ship bound for Massachusetts. When the vessel hoisted anchor, raised sails and headed out to sea, Cotton and his wife breathed a sigh of relief. Not until a month later—when the ship was half way across the Atlantic—did he reveal his identity to the passengers and crew.

JOHN COTTON

"Cotton, disguised as a seafarer, and Sarah snuck onto a ship bound for Massachusetts."

During the long ocean voyage, Sarah gave birth to a baby boy. The grateful parents called him Seaborn. Cotton said that his name was meant to remind them of the mercies they received from their gracious God on the sea.

When the ship landed in Massachusetts, word spread quickly that the famous Puritan preacher, John Cotton, was there. He happily accepted the call of the congregation in the settlement of Boston to be their minister. So he had the odd experience of fleeing his church in Boston, England, only to find himself the minister of the church in Boston, New England.

His new flock found that Cotton's preaching brought the Scriptures to life. They hung on every word. "When he preaches from the books of a prophet or apostle," one observer said, "I hear not him, I hear the very prophet and apostle. Yea, I hear the Lord Jesus Christ himself speaking in my heart."

The results of his preaching in New England were like what they had been in old England—people turned to Christ. "The presence of the Lord being mighty with him," one colonist wrote, "many souls were converted and thousands were edified."

The Cotton home became a hub of constant hospitality. Needy folks in the community and strangers arriving in Boston found a place at his table. "It was rare that his house was without a guest," a friend said. "It was a gospel inn."

Cotton, a convinced Calvinist, believed in the complete sovereignty of God in salvation. "I have read the fathers and the schoolmen and Calvin too," Cotton said, "But I find that he who has Calvin has them all."

Like other Puritans, he believed that salvation was a gift of God's free grace. Cotton was determined that his flock know that their right standing with God did not rest upon anything in them or in anything that they did. It rested only upon what Jesus Christ did for them. God's grace was everything and man's works nothing, he taught.

Cotton was so careful to give God alone the glory for saving souls that some of his hearers drew the wrong conclusion. They thought that it was not necessary for Christians to obey the law of God. One of the most outspoken of these was Anne Hutchinson. She began to gather women in her home to instruct them on the sermons that they had heard Cotton preach. Soon many of the women brought their husbands along and a large crowd came to listen to her.

Hutchinson claimed to be only teaching the things that Cotton preached, but her views were far from Cotton's and the Scripture's. Anne taught that it wasn't important to obey God's commandments. She said that John Cotton was the only minister in the colony who understood God's grace. When Anne and her followers heard other ministers preach, they stood up after the services and accused the pastors, saying, "You are teaching that people are saved by good works and not by God's grace."

As Anne Hutchinson and her followers stirred up strife, the leaders of the colony told her to stop holding meetings, but she refused. At first, Cotton defended her, accepting her claim that she was only teaching what he had preached. As time went on, Cotton discovered the depth of her errors. "The truth is," he told a friend, "many are backsliding into error and delusions. The Lord pardon them and me also who has been so slow to see it."

Eventually, Hutchinson stood before the Massachusetts court accused of disturbing the colony's peace and slandering the ministers. During the trial, Cotton pled with her to change her views. "I confess I did not know that you held any of these things," he said to her in court, "but maybe it was my lack of watchful care over you."

Despite the best efforts of Cotton and the officers of the court, she would not admit her errors. "Take heed how you proceed against me," Hutchinson warned the court, "for I know that God will ruin you and this whole state for what you do to me."

The court banished Anne Hutchinson and sixty of her followers from Massachusetts Bay Colony. Before that happened, Cotton hoped to change her mind by bringing her into his home to live with his family. Every day, he tried to show her from the Bible the error of her beliefs. At first it looked like he succeeded. She confessed her mistakes to the church, but she quickly returned to her false ideas and her harsh criticisms of the ministers. So Hutchinson and her followers had to leave the colony. Cotton was broken hearted that he failed to restore Anne to the church and community.

As Cotton studied the New Testament, he found no trace of the church hierarchy of bishops and archbishops prevalent in the Church of England. He wrote a book that argued that each local church was sovereign and had all the rights and powers that Christ gave to His church. This view was called Congregationalism or Independency. The book was widely read in England and America and it led many men to break away from the Church of England and become Congregationalists. Cotton's influence helped to make Congregationalism the preferred form of church government in New England.

In 1643, when Parliament in London took control of England from the tyranny of King Charles I, they called for a great assembly of ministers and theologians to meet at Westminster Abbey to reform the church. Members of Parliament wrote a letter to Cotton and some other leading men of the colonies, entreating them to return to England and serve on the Westminster Assembly. After much prayer, Cotton decided to remain at his post in Boston, Massachusetts.

Despite his successful ministry, John Cotton remained a humble man. He often publicly confessed his shortcomings in church with tears in his eyes. Once a drunken man, seeking to impress his friends, approached Cotton on the street and said, "You are an old fool."

"I confess I am so," Cotton replied. "May the Lord make both me and you wiser than we are—even wise unto salvation."

After church one day, a disgruntled man came up to Cotton and complained, saying, "Your ministry has become either dark or flat!"

Cotton looked the man in the eyes and answered, "Both, brother, it may be both; let me have your prayers that it may be otherwise."

When John Cotton died on December 23, 1652 at the age of sixty-eight, all of Massachusetts mourned his passing. The influence of his books and sermons lived on in England and America, and so did the legacy of his family. His eldest son Seaborn served many years as a pastor in New Hampshire. His son John learned the language of the Massachusetts Indians and preached to the Indians. Cotton's daughter, Mariah, married Increase Mather, a prominent New England minister, and she was the mother of Cotton Mather, one of the greatest preachers and theologians of colonial America.

11

ALEXANDER HENDERSON

Father of the National Covenant

(c. 1583–1646)

On a Sunday morning in July 1637, a tense crowd packed St. Giles Kirk in Edinburgh. Wealthy noblemen and the poorest of the poor thronged the church. This was the day that King Charles I had decreed that worship services in Scotland must begin to use the prayer book edited by William Laud, the Archbishop of Canterbury. For nearly seventy years, the Scots had followed a simple approach to worship that they believed was taught in the Bible. They denied that the king was the head of the church or that he had any right to interfere in the worship of the church. Ministers and noblemen from across Scotland opposed Laud's prayer book and petitioned the king to permit the Church of Scotland to worship as they believed the Bible directed them to. But Charles ignored their requests and demanded that the Scots bow to his will—even in their worship services.

The Bishop of Edinburgh and the Archbishop of St. Andrews came to St. Giles that morning to ensure that all went smoothly when the prayer book was used for the first time in the most influential church in Scotland. When a minister stood in the pulpit and began to read the opening prayer from the new worship book, the congregation began to murmur. A group of women who sat on stools at the far end of the church began to clap their hands and cry out, "Sorrow, sorrow for this sad day! They are bringing in popery among us!"

Soon the outcry echoed like a thunderclap off every stone in the old cathedral. When the frightened minister stopped reading, the bishop ordered him to proceed. Then Jenny Geddes, a poor old woman, stood up, grabbed her stool and flung it at the minister, crying, "Will you read that book in my ear?"

The congregation erupted, shouting and shoving. More stools flew. The clamor spilled out onto the streets of Edinburgh. All over the city, people protested the king's control of the church. The unrest spread to nearly every town and village in Scotland, as pent up frustrations of thirty years of interference from the Crown boiled over.

The Archbishop of St. Andrews wanted to make an example of the Scottish ministers who were the most outspoken against the prayer book. Alexander Henderson stood at the top of his list. Henderson, the pastor of a small country church in Leuchars, was Scotland's greatest defender of the independence of the church. He had written and spoken against the prayer book. Even though Henderson had nothing to do with the riot in Edinburgh, the archbishop ordered him to use the prayer book or face arrest for rebellion. Henderson hurried to Edinburgh and petitioned the king's Scottish council in Scotland to suspend the archbishop's demand. The council, flooded by petitions from every shire in Scotland, saw the folly of forcing the worship book on the Scots. They countermanded the archbishop's order and sent word to the king in London, urging him to let the Scots worship according to their own practice.

Although the council wanted to compromise, King Charles did not. He proclaimed that all who resisted the worship book were rebels. Alarmed that the king's order stripped them of any legal recourse, the Scots took a bold step. They remembered that at the time of the Reformation the Scottish people entered into a covenant which bound them to defend the Protestant faith. They decided to make a new National Covenant and asked Alexander Henderson and Archibald Johnstone to write it.

On a chilly February day in 1638, more than a thousand Scots from across the land streamed into Greyfriars Kirk in Edinburgh. The church filled to overflowing and a large crowd stood outside. Alexander Henderson led in prayer, asking God to bless what they were about to do. Then Johnstone, holding a large sheepskin parchment, read the National Covenant. The Covenant stated the primary beliefs of the Church of Scotland and the errors that they stood against. It promised to honor and defend the king but resist anything imposed on the church. When the reading ended, the people raised their right hands and vowed allegiance to the National Covenant.

Then one by one the people walked forward and signed their names. Knowing that defying the king could cost them their lives, some added "till death." A few cut their fingers and wrote with their own blood. The signing went on for hours until there was no more room on the parchment. Couriers rushed copies of the Covenant to the four corners of the land. Tens of thousands more signed. All who supported the National Covenant were called Covenanters. The Archbishop of St. Andrews, hearing how the Scottish people embraced the National Covenant, said, "In Greyfriars in one day they have thrown down what we have been building up for thirty years."

A few months later, ministers and elders of the Church of Scotland packed the High Kirk of Glasgow for their first General Assembly in twenty years. Charles's father, King James, had forced the rule of bishops on the Church of Scotland and forbade the General Assembly to meet. Charles reluctantly allowed the assembly, hoping to shape its decisions. The assembly unanimously elected Henderson moderator. King Charles sent a nobleman named Hamilton to observe the proceedings and to speak on his behalf.

The Scottish bishops who owed their positions to the king protested that the assembly was not legal and should be dismissed. The assembly rejected the protest and proceeded to bring charges against the bishops. "If you pretend to assume the right to try the bishops," Hamilton said, "then I can neither give my consent nor witness it."

With Hamilton's challenge to the assembly, the church fell silent. All eyes looked to Alexander Henderson. Henderson turned to Hamilton and said, "We are his Majesty's true and loyal subjects and we acknowledge before God our obligation to give obedience to our king. But let God, by whom kings reign, have his own place. Let Christ Jesus, the king of kings, have his own way, by whose grace our king reigns."

When Henderson took up the investigation of the bishops, the king's commissioner ordered him to stop. "No," said Henderson, "that cannot be."

"In that case," said Hamilton, "I will leave."

"Sir," said Henderson, "I wish from the bottom of my heart that you would stay, but do not obstruct the work and freedom of this assembly."

"In his Majesty's name," Hamilton said, "I hereby dissolve this assembly and forbid you to continue."

Then Hamilton marched out of the church and issued a proclamation declaring all those who remained in the assembly traitors.

Disregarding the order and threats of the king's commissioner, the General Assembly pressed on. They rejected the prayer book, removed the bishops from office and reestablished presbyterian government, undoing all that Charles and his father, King James, had forced upon the Church of Scotland. When the assembly completed their work, Henderson stood before them and said, "Now in God's abundant mercy and loving kindness He has delivered us from the chains of spiritual bondage. We must hold fast to the liberty by which Christ has set us free."

The General Assembly saw Henderson's leadership as vital to their cause. They appointed him head of the University of Edinburgh so that he could be in the capital to speak for the church. Henderson resisted for he loved his flock in Leuchars where he had pastored for nearly twenty years. "I am too old a plant," he said, "to be uprooted now."

But the assembly insisted, and he took up the work at the university. He also became the chief spokesman for the Covenanters with King Charles and the English Parliament.

After the Glasgow General Assembly, King Charles decided to crush the Scots by force of arms. When the Covenanters discovered that Charles was gathering an army to invade Scotland, they quickly formed an army of 20,000 men, trained by officers who had fought with the Protestant forces in Europe. Charles's army, without the financial backing of the English Parliament, was not up to the challenge, so the king decided it was wiser to negotiate. This began years of deceit and broken promises as Charles struggled to control the English Parliament and the Scots. One moment he told the Scots they could run the Church of Scotland as they pleased and the next he threatened to invade.

In 1641, King Charles visited Scotland and asked Alexander Henderson to be his chaplain while staying in Holyrood Palace in Edinburgh. On his first Sunday there, Charles attended the morning worship service, but did not come to the evening service. Henderson rebuked the king for not honoring the whole Lord's Day. After that, the king came to morning and evening worship. While in Edinburgh, Charles said that he would not interfere with the Church of Scotland. The king showered honors on several Scottish leaders. He made Henderson the Dean of the Chapel Royal and Archibald Johnstone a knight. But Charles was merely hoping to use the Scots in his struggle with the English Parliament. When the Scots refused to take his side against Parliament, he turned on them again.

In 1643, the Covenanters joined with the English Parliament to fight against the tyranny of King Charles. England and Scotland agreed to send their finest ministers to a great assembly in London to write a confession of faith that would unite the churches of Britain as much as possible. The Scots sent six men, including Alexander Henderson, to the Westminster Assembly. For several years, the English and Scottish ministers worked to produce the Westminster Confession of Faith and the Longer and Shorter Catechisms. These expressions of the Christian faith are the most important ever written in English and are still in use today.

In 1646, with his army nearly destroyed by the forces of the English Parliament, King Charles turned himself over to the Scottish army at Newcastle. The king immediately sent for Henderson. The Westminster Assembly believed that Henderson was the best man to convince the king to accept the reformation of the church in England and Scotland. Despite being in poor health, Henderson went to Newcastle at once. The king received him warmly, but when Henderson told him that he could be restored to his throne only if he accepted the reforms of the church, Charles refused. For six weeks, Henderson urged the king to change his mind, demonstrating from the Bible why it had been necessary to reform the church. But then Henderson's health collapsed.

He returned to Edinburgh sick, exhausted and growing weaker. Henderson knew his death was imminent. When a visitor found him smiling, he asked, "Why are you so cheerful?"

"I am hurrying to my heavenly home," Henderson answered. "Never did a schoolboy more long for play than I do to leave this world."

He died the next day on August 16, 1646. A Scottish minister said, "Alexander Henderson spent his strength and wore out his days in the service of God and the church. We will remember him as the greatest gift, after Mr. John Knox, that the Church of Scotland ever enjoyed."

Three years later, Charles I was beheaded by the English Parliament over the objections of the Scots.

12

ALEXANDER LEIGHTON

The Pilloried Puritan

(1568–c. 1643)

One February morning in 1629, while Dr. Alexander Leighton walked out of Blackfriars Church in London, a troop of armed men snatched him and pulled him away to the palace of William Laud, the Bishop of London. Bishop Laud—the king's right-hand man for church affairs—ordered him cast into Newgate prison and restrained with iron manacles. Rather than being placed in a cell, they threw Leighton into a rat-infested open pit in the prison yard. With no roof to protect him from the elements, snow, rain, and the cold winds of winter broke upon him. For fifteen weeks, officials kept him in solitary confinement, forbidding any visits from his wife and friends and refusing to provide him with a copy of the charges against him.

Alexander Leighton was born and raised in Scotland. He earned a doctorate of divinity from the University of St. Andrews and was ordained to the ministry of the Church of Scotland. Later, he graduated from medical school in the Netherlands and began to practice medicine in Utrecht where he also served as the minister of the Scottish church in the Dutch city. In the 1620s, Leighton resigned his post in Utrecht and moved to London where he intended to practice medicine. But the College of Physicians in London convinced him to join their faculty to teach aspiring doctors. Soon Leighton became known by the leading Puritans. While he was in Holland, Leighton had written a book against episcopacy—the rule of bishops—that impressed English Puritans for its scholarship, insight, and fervor. At that time, King Charles I was flexing his muscles as the head of the Church of England, installing bishops to do his bidding, and insisting that ministers and parishioners conform to his vision for the church.

In 1628, several leading Puritans, including many members of Parliament, implored Leighton to write another book against episcopacy in light of the growing abuse of power by the king's bishops. Leighton wrote *An Appeal to Parliament; or Zion's Plea Against Prelacy* in London and then traveled to Holland to get it printed. The book was intended to be read by members of Parliament to move them to rescue the nation from the tyranny of the bishops. However, while Leighton was abroad, King Charles dissolved Parliament and ruled without them. By then, about 600 copies of the book had been printed. But without the support of a sitting Parliament and knowing the persecuting zeal of the English bishops, Leighton decided to return to London without the books. However, merchants smuggled a few copies into England that soon came to the attention of Bishop Laud.

Leighton's book, highly critical of the bishops who ruled the Church of England, urged Parliament to end episcopal church government and curtail the power of the bishops. He provided many instances where the bishops abused the system for personal gain and expelled godly ministers who did not accept their unbiblical changes to the worship of the church. Like many other authors of his day, Leighton used highly charged rhetoric which was bound to inflame his enemies. Although he referred to the king respectfully, he called the bishops of the Church of England "men of blood." "We do not read of greater persecution of God's people in any nation professing the gospel," he wrote, "then in this our island, especially since the death of Queen Elizabeth."

When Laud, who was doing more than any other bishop to force high-church episcopal worship and doctrine on the church, got wind of the book, he determined to stop at nothing to silence the author and strike terror into the hearts of any who dare criticize the control

ALEXANDER LEIGHTON

"They threw Leighton into a rat-infested open pit in the prison yard."

of the church by the king and his bishops. So he ordered Leighton's arrest and trial.

While Leighton shivered in his frigid cell, agents of the court burst into his home, manhandled his wife, and held a gun to the chest of his five-year-old son, threatening to kill him if he did not tell them where his father kept his papers. Although Mrs. Leighton offered to open cabinets and boxes, they broke drawers and chests throughout the house. The officers took away anything that might be incriminating against Dr. Leighton—books, notes, and letters. But they also stole clothing and household goods.

The deplorable conditions of the prison took their toll on Leighton—shattering his strength. His hair fell out and some of his skin peeled off. When the jailor allowed a few of his physician friends to visit him, they concluded that he must have been poisoned.

Furious that Dr. Leighton had written a book against the rule of bishops, King Charles and Bishop Laud—later to become Archbishop of Canterbury—decided to make an example of Alexander Leighton. In June 1630, five months after Leighton's arrest, Laud hauled him before the Star Chamber, the secret court of the king that denied defendants the right to present witnesses or appeal the verdict. They accused him of sedition, libel, and treason. Without hearing from Leighton himself or permitting a defense to be presented on his behalf, the Star Chamber rendered a guilty verdict.

Bishop Laud called on the commissioners of the court to hand down the harshest sentence possible. They did not disappoint him. The court declared its sentence: "Leighton shall be degraded from his orders in the ministry and shall be brought to Westminster to have one of his ears cut off, one side of his nose slit and be branded on one cheek. He shall stand in the pillory and be whipped at a post. At some convenient time afterwards, he shall be carried to Cheapside on market day to have his other ear cut off, the other side of his nose slit and his other cheek branded. Then he shall be returned to prison and pay a fine of ten thousand pounds and suffer perpetual imprisonment."

When Laud heard the verdict a broad smile swept across his face, he raised his hands toward heaven and said, "Give thanks to God who has given me the victory over my enemies."

Guards led Leighton away to the Fleet prison to await punishment. Some commissioners believed that the harsh sentence would never be carried out and was meant to send a warning to anyone critical of church leaders. One knight, appalled by the severity of the sentence, approached one of the commissioners and complained that such a harsh censure set a precedent for the bishops to inflict barbaric tortures upon gentlemen. "No," the commissioner replied, "it is designed only for the terror of others. No one should think that this sentence will ever be executed."

But Bishop Laud was determined that Leighton suffer the full punishment with the utmost severity. On November 9, 1630, the night before Leighton was to be whipped and mutilated, two of his friends came to visit him in prison, sneaking in a change of clothes. Shedding his prison garb, he escaped in disguise. When the authorities discovered Leighton missing, they issued a writ of "Hue and Cry" and sent it out to the four corners of the kingdom:

A Hue and Cry against Dr. Leighton

Whereas Alexander Leighton, a Scotchman born, who was lately sentenced, by the honorable court of star-chamber, to pay a great fine to his majesty, and to undergo corporeal punishment, for writing, printing, and publishing a very libelous and seditious book against the king and his government, has escaped out of the prison of the Fleet, where he was prisoner. These are, in his majesty's name, to require and command all justices of the peace, mayors, sheriffs, bailiffs, customers, searchers, and officers of the ports, and all others, his majesty's loving subjects, to use all diligence for the apprehending of Alexander Leighton. He is a man of low stature, fair complexion; he has a yellowish beard, a high forehead, and between forty and fifty years of age.

A few days later, Leighton was captured in Bedfordshire and returned to prison. On November 26, 1630, guards led him to Westminster where they tied him to a stake. The hangman, having braced himself with hard liquor, grabbed his knife and cut off one of Leighton's ears and slit one side of his nose. Then he used a burning iron to brand his cheek with the initials *S.S.* for "Sower of Sedition." The hangman hauled him to the pillory where he locked his head and hands in the stocks and forced him to endure two hours of public mocking while snow fell and a freezing wind blew. Next, he was tied again to the post, stripped to the waist and whipped thirty-six times. Each lash cut deeply into his back. Then guards dragged him back to the prison.

Seven days later, they took Leighton to the Cheapside district of London to endure the second half of his torture. His wounds from the previous week had not begun to heal. Again the hangman tied him to the stake. He repeated the torture on the other side of his face and whipped him. Unable to walk after the ordeal, guards carried him back to prison. For ten weeks Leighton remained in the filth and cold of his unsheltered pit. Later, jailers cast him into a small cell to serve his life sentence. His punishment outraged the kingdom.

While Leighton languished in prison, Samuel Rutherford, the persecuted Scottish minister, wrote him a letter. "One day in heaven will have paid you—yea, and overpaid your blood, bonds, sorrow, and sufferings," Rutherford wrote. "O, but your hourglass of sufferings and losses, comes to little when it shall be counted and compared with the glory that abides you on the other side! I think you could wish for more ears to give than you have, since you hope these ears you now have given Him shall be passages to take in the music of His glorious voice.... I know your sufferings for Him are your glory; and therefore, weary not. His salvation is near at hand and shall not tarry."

Leighton remained in his cell for eleven years until the king called Parliament back into session in order to get Parliament to finance his wars. But Parliament immediately took steps to limit the power of King Charles and his bishops. In November 1640, Alexander Leighton appealed his sentence to Parliament. Members of the House of Commons openly wept when the details of his suffering were read aloud. They ordered that he be removed from prison to a comfortable place. When agents of Parliament brought him out of his cell, the torture and years of confinement had taken a terrible toll. He was blind, deaf, and unable to walk.

A few months later, after hearing his appeal, Parliament passed a resolution declaring that Leighton's arrest, the stealing of his papers and goods, his mutilation, torture, fine, and imprisonment were all illegal. The House of Commons voted to award Leighton six thousand pounds in reparation for his incalculable damages.

As the struggle between the king and Parliament broke down into civil war, Parliament called Laud to account for his crimes while Bishop of London and the Archbishop of Canterbury. Parliament arrested him and held him in the Tower of London for several years until his trial for high treason in 1644. On January 10, 1645, an axeman beheaded Archbishop William Laud.

13

SAMUEL RUTHERFORD

Lover of Christ

(c. 1600–1661)

One morning in late July 1636, a short thin man, carrying a bag, closed the door to his manse. Samuel Rutherford, the minister of Anwoth, a small village in southern Scotland, stepped onto the dirt road and started to walk to Edinburgh to be tried again for nonconformity. A few days before the High Commission Court in Wigton had expelled him from his church. "You are not obedient to the king and his bishops," the court declared.

Rutherford preached and wrote that the king was not the head of the Church of Scotland and had no authority to appoint bishops to rule over the church, nor dictate how the Church of Scotland should worship God. "Christ alone is the head of the church," Rutherford said. He criticized the rule of bishops and argued that the Church of Scotland should be Presbyterian—ruled by elders and ministers chosen by the people.

King Charles I had stacked the Scottish courts with judges who did his bidding. Everyone knew that a second trial in Edinburgh would confirm the decision to remove Samuel Rutherford from his church and would likely banish him from the country. "I hang by a thread," Rutherford said, "but it is of Christ's spinning."

As Rutherford trod the narrow lane from Anwoth, members of his congregation came to bid him farewell. Tears streamed down the cheeks of shepherd boys and poor cottagers who could not bear to watch their minister thrown from his church and home. For nine years he had preached to them in church and taught them as they herded sheep on the hillsides or tended their fields. "Your heaven," he told them, "would be two heavens for me, and the salvation of you all as two salvations for me."

Rutherford recognized that every day was a precious gift from God to be used wisely in the Lord's service. He rose at three o'clock each morning for prayer, Bible reading and meditation. Every day he hiked across his parish, visiting farms and cottages, never failing to be at the bedside of the sick or in the home of the grieving. He wrote books and pamphlets proclaiming the grace of God in Christ. One man said of him: "He is always praying, always preaching, always visiting the sick, always teaching, always writing and studying."

To show his congregation the beauty of Jesus Christ was the goal of all his labors. "What a flower," he exclaimed from the pulpit, "what a Rose of light and love Christ is."

"O for eternity's leisure to look on Him," he preached, "to feast upon the sight of His face! O for the long summer day of endless ages to stand beside Him and enjoy Him!"

A parishioner reported that when Rutherford preached about Christ it looked like he would fly out of the pulpit for joy.

"Every day," Rutherford said, "we may see some new thing in Christ; His love has neither brim nor bottom."

He was known to dream of Christ at night and speak of Him in his sleep.

Once a noblewoman was asked why she traveled many miles to hear Rutherford preach. "I go to Anwoth so often," she said, "because although other ministers show me the majesty of God and the plague of my own heart, Mr. Samuel does both of these things, but he also shows me as no other minister does the loveliness of Christ."

People came from great distances to hear Rutherford preach. Many visitors spent the night in his home and ate a meal at his table. One Saturday evening, a lone traveler knocked on Rutherford's door. "May I lodge here for the night?" the man asked.

Rutherford welcomed him gladly and urged him to warm himself by the fire. After supper, he asked the stranger to join them for evening devotions. Rutherford read the Bible and members of the family took turns in prayer. Then Rutherford asked the children and adults questions about the Bible. He looked to the visitor and said, "Good, sir, how many commandments are there?"

"Eleven," the stranger answered.

"Eleven?" repeated Rutherford in surprise.

"Yes—eleven," the man replied.

Rutherford told him that there were Ten Commandments. However, the stranger remained convinced that the number was eleven. Soon they all retired for the night. Rutherford went to bed astonished at the man's lack of Bible knowledge.

Early Sunday morning, Rutherford went outside to pray. As he walked the path between his house and the church, he heard a man's voice. Looking around, he saw the stranger, kneeling beneath a tree, pouring out his heart to God, asking a blessing for all who would come to worship that day. His fervent and thoughtful prayer impressed Rutherford deeply.

When the man rose from his knees, Rutherford approached him. "Are you a minister?" Samuel asked.

"I am indeed," the man replied, "I am James Ussher."

Rutherford knew his name well. Ussher was a bishop in the Protestant Church of Ireland, widely admired as one of the most learned and holy men of the day.

Ussher explained that he was passing through the area and had hoped to meet Rutherford and hear him preach. "Would you be willing to preach at Anwoth this morning?" Rutherford asked.

Ussher accepted the offer, and when he entered the pulpit, he read the Bible passage for his sermon: "A new commandment I give unto you, that you love one another." Rutherford smiled and said to himself, "Aye, there is the Eleventh Commandment."

Samuel Rutherford's joyful life at Anwoth was often gripped with sorrow. He and his wife Eupham had two children and they both died in infancy. Then his wife suffered from a long and painful illness. "She is sorely tormented night and day," he wrote. "She can't sleep, and she cries like a woman travailing in birth."

After thirteen months of agony, she died. "An afflicted life looks very like the way that leads to the kingdom," he said. "The Lord has done it; blessed be His name."

After his wife and children died, Rutherford lived alone in the manse with his widowed mother. Then she, too, fell gravely ill. "My mother is weak, and I think shall leave me alone," Rutherford wrote a friend, "but I am not alone, because Christ's Father is with me."

A few weeks later, she died. Through his grief he clung to God. "Welcome, cross of Christ, if Christ be with it," he wrote after his mother's death.

Sorrows made him long for heaven. "I am a man often borne down and hungry," he said, "and waiting for the marriage supper of the Lamb."

Rutherford knew that God used difficulties for the good of His children to teach them valuable lessons, and he strove to find God's gifts hidden in his trials. "When I am in the cellar of affliction," he said, "I look for the Lord's choicest wines."

Although the people liked Rutherford, few, at first, put their trust in Christ. After two years in Anwoth, he wrote, "I see exceedingly small fruit of my ministry. I would be glad of one soul to be my crown of joy in the day of Christ."

But he pressed on and trusted God for the salvation of their souls. He never doubted that he was right where the Lord wanted him to be. "The Great Master Gardener in a wonderful providence planted me here," Rutherford wrote a friend, "and here I will abide until the Master of the Vineyard think fit to transplant me."

Through the years, many of them did believe in Jesus Christ, and Christ transformed their lives.

Several members of the Anwoth church went to Edinburgh with Rutherford, and encouraged him at his three-day trial. But in the end, the court declared him an enemy of the king. It forbade him to preach anywhere in Scotland and banished him to Aberdeen, a city hundreds of miles to the north. The court refused to give him time to return to Anwoth to collect his things and say goodbye. Although confined to Aberdeen, he was free to move about the city, however, he was not to leave Aberdeen under pain of death. Being torn from his flock crushed him. "They are dear to my soul," he wrote a friend about his congregation in Anwoth. "The memory of them breaks my heart."

When the bishop sent a new minister to Anwoth who supported the rule of bishops, the congregation loudly protested and refused to have him. Anwoth's pulpit remained empty. The people of Anwoth prayed fervently for the return of their pastor.

At first, the citizens of Aberdeen turned a cold shoulder to Rutherford, but over time, he won friends. They called him "the banished minister." However, out of fear for the authorities, most of them spoke with him in secret. "I find folks here are kind to me," he wrote after a few months, "but in the night and under their breath."

Gradually, a few families asked him to teach Bible studies in their homes. When the local ministers and theologians found out about it, they tried to discredit him, publicly condemning Rutherford's teachings and challenging him to a series of debates. But it backfired. Rutherford crushed their arguments with his knowledge of the Bible and his quick wit. After being drubbed in three debates, they were afraid to take him on again. As Rutherford's ideas won favor among more and more people, Aberdeen officials demanded that King Charles banish Rutherford from the kingdom altogether. But no such order ever came.

Being far from his home and his people compelled Rutherford to lean on Christ as never before. "He was always kind to my soul," he wrote from Aberdeen, "but never so kind as now in my greatest distress."

The preaching ban was the greatest blow of all. Rutherford called his Lord's Days in Aberdeen "my silent Sabbaths."

During his exile, Rutherford wrote letters—hundreds of letters—to believers across Scotland. He wrote his friends to deepen their love for Jesus Christ and strengthen their faith. Many recipients circulated the letters to others to encourage them.

In 1638, ministers of the Scottish church and many noblemen rose up to break the king's domination over the church and the state. Within a few months, believers throughout Scotland resisted the king's claim to be the head of the church. They signed a National Covenant, pledging to restore biblical worship and church government to the Church of Scotland. The supporters of the National Covenant became known as Covenanters. When Rutherford learned of it, he risked all and left Aberdeen, preaching as he made his way home. There was great rejoicing in Anwoth when, after a two-year exile, Rutherford led his flock in worship again.

A few months later, Rutherford served at the General Assembly of the Church of Scotland in Glasgow. The assembly took away the power of the king's bishops and restored presbyterian government to the Scottish church. The delegates, recognizing that Rutherford was one of the holiest and most learned ministers in Scotland, decided to send him to University of St. Andrews to train men to be pastors. Rutherford urged the assembly to let him remain at Anwoth, but they refused. "My removal from my flock is so heavy to me," he wrote, "that I never had such a longing for death."

At St. Andrews, Rutherford threw himself into shaping the hearts and minds of young men for the ministry. Years later, one former student described St. Andrews University under Rutherford's leadership: "It became a Lebanon out of which were taken cedars for building the House of the Lord throughout the whole land."

Ten years after his wife died, Rutherford married for a second time. His new wife Jean was a godly woman. One man who knew them well wrote, "I never knew any among men exceed him, nor any among women exceed her."

Samuel and Jean had seven children, but their home life was often taken up with nursing the sick and burying the dead. All but one of their children died before reaching adulthood. His family sufferings enabled Rutherford to comfort others who lost loved ones. He told the grieving that Christ was with them in their suffering. "You are not your own but bought with a price,' he said, "and your sorrow is not your own."

In 1643, the English Parliament, controlled by Puritans, organized a great assembly of the leading pastors and theologians to meet in Westminster Abbey in London to reform and unite the churches of Britain. They asked Scotland to participate. The Church of Scotland sent several of their finest men, including Samuel Rutherford. For four years, Rutherford helped to write the Westminster Confession of Faith and the Shorter and Longer Catechisms. He lived and worked with the English Puritans and grew to appreciate them. "I judge," he wrote, "that in England the Lord has a fair company that shall stand at the side of Christ in His kingdom."

While in London, Rutherford wrote *Lex Rex*, a book about the power and place of kings. Unlike the kings of England who claimed that they had a right from God to rule as they pleased, Rutherford argued that God is the ultimate ruler of the kingdom. God entrusted earthly authority in the people and the king was empowered to work for the good of the people. "The law is king," Rutherford wrote, not some power-hungry monarch. His book took England and Scotland by storm. Soon it was read throughout Europe. Rutherford's passionate call for limited government shaped political thought in Britain and later in America for generations.

When Rutherford left the Westminster Assembly, the English members wrote a letter to the Church of Scotland: "We restore him to you with gratitude for his learning, godliness, faithfulness, and diligence. We humbly pray that our heavenly Father will increase the number of such burning and shining lights among you."

Rutherford returned to St. Andrews to teach at the university and to preach. He never left Scotland again, although the fame of his books led to several offers of professorships from universities in Europe.

In 1649, the English Parliament put to death King Charles I. His son Prince Charles fled the country. Most Scots bitterly opposed the killing of Charles I. They thought his son should be crowned king, if he pledged not to interfere with the Church of Scotland.

Prince Charles needed the support of the Scots to regain the throne in England. He promised to protect the independence of the Scottish church and to grant a strong voice for the people in government. When he visited St. Andrews in 1650, Rutherford gave a speech on the duty of kings to love God and serve the people. Charles did nothing at the time, but he marked out Rutherford for revenge in the future.

When, in May of 1660, Charles was crowned King Charles II in London, he immediately broke all his promises to the Scottish people. He seated a Scottish parliament loyal only to him. Impoverished Scottish nobles did the king's bidding in exchange for land and titles. Step by step, they made Charles II absolute ruler of Scotland and abolished all the laws supporting the independence of the Church of Scotland. Bishops appointed by the Crown took control of the churches again, and attacked outspoken Covenanters like

Rutherford. They condemned *Lex Rex* as treason. The hangman burned copies of it at the Mercat Cross in Edinburgh. A bonfire, fueled by copies of *Lex Rex*, was lit below Rutherford's window at St. Andrews University.

The Parliament removed him from his post and confined him to his rooms at the college. Not long after, they sent a summons, ordering him to appear before Parliament to stand trial for high treason. They planned to put him to death in Edinburgh. When messengers delivered the summons, Rutherford was gravely ill, near death. He wished he had the strength to stand trial, but he did not. Rutherford propped himself up in bed and said to the messengers, "Tell them that I have a summons already from a superior Judge, and I must answer my first summons; and, ere your day arrives, I will be where few kings and great folks come."

The Scottish Parliament ordered that he should not be permitted to die on the grounds of the university. One courageous member stood and said, "You have voted that honest man out of his college, but you cannot vote him out of heaven."

"I think it would be a more glorious way of going home," Rutherford said, "to lay down my life for the cause of Christ at the Cross of Edinburgh; but I submit to my Master's will."

As his strength failed, a friend asked him, "What do you think of Christ now?"

"I shall live and adore Him," Rutherford answered, "Glory, glory to my Creator and Redeemer forever."

"Think of all your good works and sufferings for the Lord," one visitor told him.

"I disclaim all!" Rutherford shot back. "Let my name be ground to pieces that Christ may be all in all."

His last words before he died on March 20, 1661 were "Glory, glory dwelleth in Emmanuel's land!"

After his death, a friend collected more than three hundred of Rutherford's letters and printed them in a book. Few Christian books have been so widely read and so greatly loved. Richard Baxter, a Puritan pastor and theologian, said of Rutherford's letters, "Except for the Bible, such a book the world never saw."

In 1857, Anne Cousin wove phrases from Rutherford's letters into a hymn called "The Sands of Time are Sinking." It is still widely sung today.

The sands of time are sinking,
The dawn of heaven breaks,
The summer morn I've sighed for,
The fair sweet morn awakes;
Dark, dark hath been the midnight,
But dayspring is at hand,
And glory, glory dwelleth in Emmanuel's land.

14

JAMES GUTHRIE

That Short Man Who Could Not Bow

(c. 1616–1661)

It was 1638 in Scotland and a young minister named James Guthrie paced up and down nervously. He had come to sign the National Covenant to support the liberty of the Church of Scotland against the encroachments of the king. But on his way to sign the document, he walked by the town's hangman. The sight of the hangman served as a fearful reminder that all who placed their signature on the National Covenant might well be signing their own death warrants. As others stepped forward to sign, Guthrie prayed, fidgeted, and walked about. After a while he mustered the courage to write his name. After this halting beginning, Guthrie never wavered, becoming a staunch defender of Christ's church, defying the king and all others who sought to dominate it. One man called him, "That short man who could not bow."

As a young teacher of philosophy at St. Andrews University, Guthrie was inspired to become a Presbyterian minister by the saintly Samuel Rutherford. He met weekly with Rutherford and other professors for Bible study and prayer. Rutherford's clear Bible teaching and deep love for Christ captured Guthrie's heart. Looking back on that time, he said, "I am not ashamed to give glory to God that I was treading other steps then; and the Lord did graciously recover me."

He left St. Andrews and began his life's work as a pastor in Stirling, preaching and caring for his flock. Highly-educated aristocrats and poor cottagers alike understood his sermons which centered on Christ and his sacrifice on the cross. Through many years of ministry, his deep devotion for Christ never waned. "He always had the joy of the Lord of a young convert," his church assistant said.

The ministers of the Church of Scotland often called upon James Guthrie to lead during those difficult years of the church's struggle with the king.

In 1650, with the support of Scottish nobles and ministers, Charles II was crowned king at Scone. He pledged not to interfere in matters of the church and swore allegiance to the National Covenant and the Solemn League and Covenant. But Charles, a conniving and dishonest man, quickly broke his promise to respect the freedom of the church. The king and his council, upset with a position on a church matter that Guthrie and his fellow minister David Bennet had taken, ordered that they appear before them. Guthrie and Bennet wrote to the king and his council, "We do acknowledge the king and your lordships are the lawful civil authority of the land to whom we are most willing to give obedience. But we believe that the courts of the church are the only proper judges of our doctrine and our ministerial calling. We do not acknowledge that his Majesty and your lordships are the proper judges of those things. We have a tender regard to hold fast to the liberties and privileges of the Church of Jesus Christ."

Their stand infuriated the king. He decided not to press the matter at that time, but he did not forget it. Ten years later, Guthrie would pay for it.

In 1660, the year that Charles II gained the throne in England, James Guthrie and eleven other churchmen wrote to the king. They expressed their delight that Charles now reigned over all of Britain and promised their loyalty. But they reminded the king of his pledge to protect the religious liberty of the church. "It is the desire of our souls that your Majesty may be like David, a man after God's own heart," they wrote, "like Solomon with an understanding heart to judge the Lord's people; like Josiah who was tender-hearted and humbled himself before God."

The letter did not move King Charles II to honor his promise or to rule righteously. Instead, he ordered the men imprisoned in Edinburgh Castle. While Guthrie languished in prison, Samuel Rutherford sent him a letter, encouraging him to hold fast to God's truth. "Think it not strange that men devise against you," Rutherford wrote, "whether it be to exile, the earth is the Lord's; or perpetual imprisonment, the Lord is your light and liberty; or a violent and public death, for the kingdom of heaven consists in a fair company of glorified martyrs and witnesses of whom Jesus Christ is the chief witness. Happy are you if you give testimony to the world of your preferring Jesus Christ to all powers."

Rutherford closed the letter by encouraging Guthrie to entrust everything into the hands of his faithful Savior. "Cast the burden of wife and children on the Lord Christ," he advised. "He cares for you and them. Your blood is precious in His sight."

A few months later, the Scottish Parliament, under orders from the king, put Guthrie on trial for high treason. The indictment accused Guthrie of plotting to destroy the king's government.

James Guthrie spoke in his own defense, citing acts of Parliament and decrees of the king to demonstrate that he had simply exercised the rights of ministers of the Church of Scotland. He argued that far from being a traitor to the king, he had been his advocate. He had protested the killing of the king's father, Charles I, and supported the restoration of Charles II to the throne. He asserted that his writing and preaching defended the National Covenant and the Solemn League and Covenant which Charles II had sworn to uphold.

He closed by saying, "My conscience I cannot submit, but this old crazy body and mortal flesh I do submit, to do with whatever you will, whether by death, or banishment, or imprisonment, or anything else."

After hearing Guthrie's defense, several members of Parliament declared that they would have nothing to do with putting to death the righteous man, but most called for his blood. Parliament found him guilty of treason. The clerk read aloud the sentence: "Mr. James Guthrie is to be hanged at the Cross of Edinburgh and his head is to be affixed on the Netherbow Port in the city of Edinburgh, and his lands and goods confiscated." Guthrie accepted the sentence with a calm and cheerful spirit.

Guards locked him away in the Tolbooth prison to await his execution. There, he met the doomed-to-die Marquis of Argyll. If Guthrie was the most fearless Covenanting minister, Argyll was its bravest nobleman. Argyll had crowned Charles II at Scone, and backed his claim to the throne of England. But in 1660 when Argyll traveled to London to celebrate Charles' coronation, Charles had him arrested and thrown in the Tower of London. Eventually, the king sent him to Edinburgh for trial. The court did the king's bidding by sentencing Argyll to death. "I had the honor to set the crown on the king's head," Argyll said, "and now he hastens me to a better crown than his own."

"Such is my respect for your Lordship," Guthrie told Argyll in prison, "that were I not under the sentence of death myself I could cheerfully die for you."

The hangman beheaded Argyll a few days later. The morning of his execution, Argyll wrote his daughter-in-law: "What shall I say in this great day of the Lord, where in the midst of a cloud, I have found a fair sunshine. I can wish no more for you, but that the Lord may comfort you, and shine upon you as He does upon me, and give you that same sense of His love in staying in the world, as I have in going out of it."

Later, when Guthrie's wife came to visit he said, "I am more fortunate than the Marquis of Argyll for he was beheaded, but I am to be hanged on a tree as my Savior was."

His wife brought their young daughter and five-year-old son William to see him. "Willie," Guthrie said, lifting the boy into his arms, "the day will come when they will cast up to you that your father was hanged. But don't be ashamed, lad. It is in a good cause."

James Guthrie arose early the morning of his execution and spent a long time in prayer. A friend who stayed with him in the cell said, "His face seemed truly to shine." His friend asked, "How are you doing?"

"Very well," he said. "This is the day which the Lord hath made, let us be glad and rejoice in it."

Guthrie wrote his wife a final letter: "My heart, being within a few hours of laying down my life for the testimony of Jesus Christ, I send you these few lines as the last act of spotless affection which I bear to you. To me you have been a very kind and faithful helper in the work of the Lord. God will watch over you and our children whom

I leave to your care to bring them up in the knowledge of the Lord. Let not your wants and weaknesses discourage you; there are power, riches, and abundance with God, and He will supply all your wants and carry you through. Give yourself to prayer, and be diligent in reading the Holy Scriptures. My heart! May Jesus Christ be all your salvation and all your desire!"

Guards led him from the prison to the scaffold. He handed a copy of the speech he hoped to deliver from the scaffold to a friend and asked him to give it to his son when he was older.

As he stood at the top of the scaffold next to the hangman's rope, he looked over the vast crowd gathered below him and said, "I acknowledge that I am a sinner and one of the most unworthy men that has ever preached the gospel. But I do believe that Jesus Christ came into the world to save sinners of whom I am the chief. I have preached salvation through His name. I commend to you the riches of His free grace for the only way you can be saved is through faith in Christ. I would not exchange this scaffold for the palace and mitre of the greatest prelate in Britain."

As the hangman wrapped the noose around his neck, Guthrie prayed, "O my Holy One—I shall not die, but live. Now let your servant depart in peace for my eyes have seen your salvation."

Afterward, the king's men stuck Guthrie's head on an iron spike and fastened it to the highest point of the Netherbow gate in Edinburgh. They meant it to serve as a warning to anyone who challenged the king's authority in the church. Instead, Guthrie's example inspired many Scots to hold fast to the Covenants. Guthrie's son, Willie, often walked to the gate and looked up at his father's head. He followed in his father's footsteps and became a Christian minister. James Guthrie's skull hung above the gate for twenty-seven years until Sandie Hamilton, a young Covenanter, bravely climbed the tall Netherbow, brought it down, and gave it a proper burial.

15

JOHN OWEN

Prince of Puritan Theologians

(1616–1683)

In 1642, twenty-six-year-old John Owen wallowed in dark depression. King Charles I tried to rule Britain by divine right and control the church. Parliament and the English Puritans resisted his abuse of power, and civil war erupted. Owen's Puritan convictions got him run out of Oxford University and the academic life he loved. He had just been fired from his position as a chaplain because the nobleman he served sided with the king, and Owen favored Parliament. His wealthy uncle, a staunch defender of the king who had paid for Owen's expenses while he earned degrees at Oxford, had just disowned him.

With no job, no money and little hope, Owen went to London where he had relatives.

John Owen believed the doctrines of the Christian faith intellectually, but the guilt of his sins plagued his thoughts. He lacked the assurance that he was a forgiven child of God. In London, fears and doubts so overpowered him that he hardly said a word to anyone for three months. When he did speak, his words were so incoherent that people thought he was losing his mind.

Then one Sunday, Owen went with his cousin to hear a famous preacher. When they arrived at the church, they found many people leaving the building. Soon they discovered that the well-known minister was not going to be speaking after all. "Let's go down the road and hear another preacher," his cousin suggested.

"No," Owen answered, "I'm tired and I don't want to walk any further. Let's stay here for the service."

A country minister, unknown to the congregation, stepped into the pulpit and read the text of his sermon from Matthew Chapter 8, "Why are you fearful? O you of little faith!"

Owen sat bolt upright in the pew. "This is a message for me," he said to himself. He prayed a silent prayer, asking God to bless the sermon to his heart. The minister spoke directly to many of the fears which Owen had about his own weak faith. Although not profound or eloquent, the message pointed Owen to Christ and away from himself. He left the church filled with confidence in Christ's love and mercy for him.

John Owen was a changed man, and it led to a changed life. Before, he had no peace, no direction, and no calling, now, energized by his renewed faith; he threw himself into serving the Lord. Realizing that his peace with God was a gift from God alone and not a result of anything that he had done, he wrote a book proclaiming God's sovereign control over all things—especially the salvation of every believer.

After reading Owen's book, members of Parliament appointed him to be the minister of the long-neglected congregation in Fordham. Owen poured his efforts into serving his new flock. "I desire to be a servant to you in the work of the Lord," he told them, "and to do all I can to help you and your families."

His sermons drew the people to Christ alone for the forgiveness of their sins. And he challenged them, by the grace of God, to live holy lives. They soon grew used to the sight of their tall minister visiting from house to house, encouraging his people in their faith and comforting the sick. "He was serious and cheerful and easy to talk to," said one who knew him well. "He spoke often of heaven and loving Christ and His saints."

"My heart's desire is that you may be saved," he told his congregation. "I have great heaviness and continual sorrow in my heart for those who do not walk according to the gospel."

"It was the purpose of God," Owen preached, "that His Son should offer a sacrifice of infinite worth and dignity. If there were a thousand worlds, the gospel might on this ground be preached to all of them, if they will only believe in Him."

His biblical preaching and his evident love for them won their hearts. Many came to faith in Christ, and Owen called them to live in obedience to God's commandments. "Let none," he said, "pretend that they love the people of God while they do not love fervently those who are in their church with them. I would rather see a church filled with love a thousand times, than filled with the best, the highest, and most glorious gifts."

In April of 1646, he accepted an invitation to preach to Parliament in London. The members of the House of Commons crowded into St. Margaret's Church in the shadow of Westminster Abbey to hear John Owen. His sermon praised God's free mercy and grace to undeserving sinners. "Labor to let all parts of the kingdom know the gospel of the Lord Jesus!" he told them,

Parliament had his message printed and circulated throughout the land. Owen was fast becoming one of the most famous ministers in England.

Later, he accepted a call to the church in Coggeshall, a large congregation of 2,000 souls. During this time, Owen married Mary Rooke. They had eleven children, but sorrow and grieving were never far from their door. All but one of their children died in infancy or early youth. None survived their parents.

While ministering in Coggeshall, John Owen concluded that local congregations should not be under the spiritual authority of bishops, archbishops or kings. He believed that each congregation should be independent, answerable to its own elected leadership. Owen became a leader of the nonconformists, those that did not follow the Church of England's requirements to conform to their doctrine, worship, and government. He wrote books defending the right of nonconformists to follow Christ in the ways that they believed the Bible directed them.

Despite a demanding schedule of preaching and visiting his large flock, Owen wrote book after book. Among his most important was *The Death of Death in the Death of Christ,* which explained in great detail the work of Christ's sacrifice on the cross to redeem guilty sinners, demonstrating from the Scriptures that everyone for whom Christ died would be saved. No one could snatch Christ's own people out of His hand.

By the summer of 1648, the Parliamentary Army had crushed the king's forces and took King Charles prisoner. On the last day of January in 1649, Parliament asked Owen to preach to them again. The day before, Parliament had executed Charles for treason. In his sermon, Owen did not mention the execution of the king. He told the Parliament, "Much of the evil which had come upon the country had originated within your own walls." He warned them against "oppression, self-seeking, and persecution."

Oliver Cromwell, the greatest general of Parliament's army and a member of the House of Commons, heard Owen and was impressed. He asked Owen to come with him when he brought the army to Ireland to suppress an uprising. The Catholics in Ireland had made an alliance with English Royalists to invade England and place on the throne Prince Charles, the son of the executed King Charles. Owen told Cromwell that he could not leave his church, but he refused to take no for an answer. Cromwell wrote to the church at Coggeshall and told them that Owen must come with him to Ireland. And so began John Owen's close connection with Oliver Cromwell, the most powerful man in England.

The Army of the Commonwealth or the New Model Army, as it was called after the execution of the king, was a well-disciplined army known for its earnest Christian faith. Many of the soldiers spent their free time reading the Bible, praying, and singing psalms. "I saw a great deal of piety in the commanders and soldiers of the parliament's army;" a royalist leader said, "but I can find little godliness in our own men."

In Ireland, John Owen reorganized Trinity College in Dublin and preached to large crowds of Irishmen hungry for the good news of Jesus. One woman who became a Christian under Owen's preaching there said, "Mr. Owen was the first man by whose ministry I became sensible of my condition. I was cast down and had no rest within me. He bid me believe in Christ, and be fervent in prayer."

Another man said, "I heard Mr. Owen in Dublin. He did me much good and made me to see my misery and my need of Christ."

In 1651, Oliver Cromwell became chancellor of Oxford University. However, since he was busy with the army, he delegated his rule over the university to John Owen, whom he made vice chancellor. So Owen resigned from his ministry in Coggeshall and moved to Oxford. During the Civil War, the king had made Oxford his headquarters. The king's troops had used college halls as barracks for soldiers and stables for horses. Owen found some of the colleges closed and all of them in disarray. He faced a daunting job of restoring the university to its former condition. Owen stated his goal for the university: "That the gospel of our Lord and Savior Jesus Christ may be adorned in all things."

Owen preached every other Sunday at St. Mary's, the University Church of Oxford. One of his hearers wrote, "He had a very graceful and winning way in the pulpit. He moves and wins the affections of his hearers."

Together with his wife, Owen offered hospitality to students in his home. He sponsored a number of poorer students with his own money to enable them to attend college. Many Oxford students traced their deepened faith in Christ to Owen's sermons and his Christian example.

Owen admired and served Cromwell. But he stood against him when it was in the best interests of the nation. When Cromwell considered taking the title of king, Owen wrote a petition urging him not to take the crown. In the end, Cromwell agreed not to become king. When Richard Cromwell succeeded his father as chancellor of Oxford, he stripped Owen of his responsibilities at Oxford University. John Owen spent most of the rest of his life in London writing and preaching.

In 1660, when Charles II was restored to the throne of his father, he sought to control the church with a stronger grip than his father had. A time of fierce religious persecution began. Hundreds of ministers who refused to submit to the king's demands regarding worship were cast out of their churches. No one could preach without a license from the king. Religious meetings that occurred outside of approved churches were declared illegal.

Believing that he must obey God rather than men, Owen did not submit to the king's laws against unauthorized preaching. He preached at secret gatherings in London and elsewhere. Once, the authorities raided his home while he was preaching and charged him with holding an illegal worship service. But John Owen never landed in prison because influential supporters protected him. Owen used his connections to try to get his friends released from prison, including John Bunyan.

When a deadly plague swept through London in 1666, tens of thousands fled the city, including most of the licensed ministers, leaving the sick to fend for themselves. Owen and other nonconformist ministers stayed to help the ill and the dying. On the heels of the plague came a horrendous fire which destroyed most of the buildings and churches of London. Nonconformist ministers set up temporary places of worship and preached to the devastated people. For a time, Owen and other nonconformists were permitted to have public services, but before long the king forbade it again.

When John Bunyan was released from jail in 1676, he met Owen in London. Bunyan showed him the manuscript of *The Pilgrim's Progress,* which he had written while in prison. Although Bunyan was a tinker, a repairman of metal utensils, with little schooling, Owen recognized the genius of the work immediately. He told Bunyan to bring it to his publisher. Owen's publisher printed it, and soon *The Pilgrim's Progress* was read throughout the kingdom.

Owen admired Bunyan's preaching too. Whenever Bunyan preached in London, Owen listened to him proclaim the good news of Jesus Christ. Once when Owen met with the king, the king asked him, "Why do you go to hear an uneducated tinker?"

"I would gladly give up all my learning," Owen told the king, "if I could have the tinker's gift for preaching."

Over the last forty years of his life, Owen wrote dozens of books—books on theology, books on Christian devotion, books on religious liberty, Bible commentaries, and more. In his writings, he meticulously examined a topic in great detail to cover every possible angle. Owen believed that the central theme of the Old and New Testament was the person and work of Jesus Christ. "We only understand the Scriptures as much as we know the sufferings and glory of Christ," he wrote.

"Christ is our best friend," he once said, "and before long He will be our only friend."

A major theme of his writings was the believer's fight against sin. He knew that it was vital for every Christian to understand the power of indwelling sin. "Let our hearts admit," Owen wrote, "'I am poor and weak. Satan is too subtle, too cunning, and too powerful; he watches constantly for advantages over my soul. Occasions and opportunities for temptation are innumerable. No wonder I do not know how deeply involved I have been with sin. Therefore, on God alone will I rely for my keeping. I will continually look to Him.'"

"Be killing sin or it will be killing you," warned Owen.

Near the end of his life, when he finished writing a massive four-volume commentary on the book of Hebrews, he told a friend, "Now my work is done: it is time for me to die."

He died in 1683 at the age of sixty-seven and was buried in Bunhill Fields in London. A few years later, his friend John Bunyan was laid to rest near him in the same graveyard. Friends had inscribed on Owen's tombstone: "He held up to all who were set out for heaven the lamp of evangelical truth to guide their steps to immortal glory."

16

JOHN GIFFORD AND JOHN BUNYAN

Evangelist and Pilgrim

(Bunyan: 1628–1686)

On June 2, 1648, the first rays of sun lit the streets and fields of Maidstone, England. Throughout the day and night before, the army of Parliament had crushed a large force loyal to King Charles I. Hundreds of bodies lay dead in the streets. The wounded groaned. More than one thousand exhausted royalist soldiers hid in the hop fields and woods on the edge of town. The morning light revealed that they were completely surrounded. With no hope of rescue, the soldiers of the king surrendered.

The Battle of Maidstone was one of the last of the English Civil War, leaving King Charles I defeated and Parliament ruling the land. Parliament later released all of the royalist prisoners from the battle, except twelve of the leaders who were sentenced to hang. Among them was Major John Gifford.

The night before Gifford's execution, his sister came to visit him. She found the guard at the door fast asleep and the rest of the watch in a drunken stupor. "This is your chance," she told Gifford. "Make your escape and save your life."

Slipping past the dozing guards and out into the darkness, Gifford ran across fields and crept into a narrow ditch. He lay there three days while soldiers scoured the countryside for him. He dared not return to his home in Kent for fear of capture, so with the help of royalist friends, he hid out for months. In time, he settled in Bedford, a small town where no one knew him.

John Gifford, a loud, immoral drunkard who swore constantly, made a mess of his new life in Bedford. He despised Christians and made his disdain known to all. His hatred for Anthony Harrington, an outspoken Christian of the town, led Gifford to boast that he would kill Harrington one day.

The money Gifford made, he quickly lost through gambling. His gambling losses cast him into fits of despair. Many times he resolved to quit gambling, but the addiction always overpowered him. One night after losing a large sum of money, Gifford threw himself into a rage, cursing God and blaming the Almighty for his troubles. In the midst of his tirade, he was struck dumb when he heard the blasphemy spewing from his mouth and caught a glimpse of the evil in his heart. For weeks, he suffered under the crushing weight of his sin and guilt. Out of desperation, he began to read the Bible, and he discovered the forgiveness of sins promised to all who come to Jesus Christ.

John Gifford's life turned upside down. He stopped drinking and gambling and cursing. He discovered a love for others that he had never felt before. When he learned about a small group of Christians—that included Anthony Harrington—who met for Bible study and prayer, he asked to join them. At first they put him off. "He has been so vile and done such wild things in town," they said to one another. They remembered his threats to kill Harrington. But Gifford wouldn't take no for an answer. Time and again he asked to come to their meetings. His persistence wore them down, and they reluctantly agreed to let him come. From the start, they could tell he was a heartfelt Christian who soaked in the Word of God like a sponge. Before long, Gifford was leading the Bible study, clearly explaining the Scriptures and applying them to everyday life.

In 1650, when the small group of believers in Bedford decided to form an independent congregation, they agreed unanimously to call John Gifford as their first pastor. The Christians of Bedford called him "Holy Mr. Gifford." At this time, there was no king—Parliament and Oliver Cromwell ruled the land. Cromwell allowed Protestant Christian groups to worship freely. Nonconformist and

Independent congregations, which had been persecuted during the reign of Charles I, began to thrive. Cromwell's government granted Gifford's small congregation the use of the chapel of St. John's Hospital in Bedford.

The little congregation grew slowly, but what they lacked in numbers, they made up for in zeal. John Gifford's winsome preaching and his wise counsel deepened the faith of his flock.

Now there was a tinker from the nearby village of Elstow who often came to Bedford to mend pots and pans. His name was John Bunyan. Like Gifford, he had been widely known as a crude man, full of cursing and folly. But he had started reading religious books and going to his parish church. He took an oath to stop swearing—and stuck to it. His neighbors, amazed by the change, praised him for it. "I please God as well as any man in England," he said to himself.

One day, as Bunyan walked along a street in Bedford—his anvil on his back and tool box in hand—he saw some women sitting on a porch in the sun. He overheard them talking about their relationship with God. "I drew near to hear what they said," Bunyan said later, "for I, too, was now a brisk talker in the matters of religion."

The women's conversation stunned him. They said that in themselves they could do nothing good, and that they were saved only through the righteousness of Christ. The women rejoiced that they had been born again through faith in Jesus. "I heard them," Bunyan said, "but I did not understand them; for they were far above me. They spoke as if joy made them speak. They spoke with such pleasantness of Scripture language and with such appearance of grace in all they said, that they were to me as if they had found a new world."

Realizing that he had been playing religious games, Bunyan left, his chest pounding and his spiritual pride shattered. "They were on the sunny side of some high mountain, refreshing themselves with the pleasant beams of the sun," he said of the women, "while I was shivering under a dark cloud in the frost and snow."

As the weeks passed, Bunyan often went to see the Bedford women. They read the Scriptures to him and urged him to put his trust in Jesus Christ. "You need to talk to our pastor," they said. So they walked him across town and introduced him to John Gifford. The stout old Gifford gripped his hand warmly and invited him in. They talked for hours. Again and again, he met with Gifford for counsel, prayer, and Bible study.

He began attending Gifford's church, but doubts plagued him for a long time. Once he went to worship worried that Christ would never accept him. Gifford preached about the undying love of Christ for sinners. "These words did suddenly break in upon me," Bunyan said later, "'My grace is sufficient for you, My grace is sufficient for you, My grace is sufficient for you,' three times together; and I thought that every word was a mighty word unto me."

"Christ! Christ! There was nothing but Christ before my eyes," Bunyan declared. "Now Christ was my all; all my wisdom, all my righteousness, all my sanctification, and all my redemption." Bunyan walked home, his heart overflowing. "I could have spoken of His love and mercy to me, even to the crows who sat upon the ploughed land before me," he said.

Bunyan started to lead others to Christ. In 1655, two hard blows fell upon Bunyan: his wife died and left him alone to care for their four children, and not long after, John Gifford passed away. Gifford, in a letter to his congregation written from his deathbed, exhorted his flock to walk together in love when he was gone. "You were not joined to the ministry," he reminded them, "but to Christ and the Church. Stand fast; the Lord is at hand."

The congregation sent men from the church, including Bunyan, to preach in the nearby villages. Bunyan proved to be an effective preacher. "I had not preached long," Bunyan wrote, "before some began to be greatly afflicted in their minds with the greatness of their sin and of their need for Jesus Christ."

Soon large crowds came to hear him preach. Although he kept earning his living as a tinker, he spent more and more time preaching. John Bunyan married a Christian woman named Elizabeth who loved his children as her own. Elizabeth gave birth to two more children. The Bunyan home brimmed with laughter and joy.

Everything changed in 1660 when King Charles II came to the throne. He wanted to force everyone in the kingdom, regardless of conscience, to worship using the Book of Common Prayer in their local Church of England congregation. Those who failed to attend their parish church faced fines or imprisonment. Laws were passed making it illegal for nonconformists like Bunyan to preach or gather for worship. One evening, when Bunyan began to preach to some poor farmers in a country cottage, the constable and his deputies barged in and seized him. As they pulled him away, Bunyan told the congregation, "It is a mercy of God to suffer for doing good. Better by far to be the persecuted than the persecutors."

The next morning the constable hauled Bunyan before a judge, who asked him, "Why do you go to such meetings and preach?"

"I went," Bunyan replied, "to instruct the people to forsake their sins and trust in Christ."

"But you are a tinker," the judge said, "why don't you follow your trade? It is unlawful for you to carry on religious services as you do."

"I do follow my calling and preach the Word too," Bunyan answered.

"I will send you to jail unless you promise to stop preaching," the judge said.

"I shall not stop speaking the Word of God," Bunyan said. "I shall continue to counsel, comfort, and teach the people that desire it."

"Don't you love your wife and children?" asked the judge.

"Indeed I do, very dearly," Bunyan said, his heart breaking at the thought of leaving his family, "but in comparison with Jesus Christ I do not love them at all."

The judge ordered him held in jail to be tried at the next meeting of the county court.

Two months passed before Bunyan stood before a panel of judges. A clerk read the charge. "John Bunyan of the town of Bedford, laborer, has devilishly and perniciously abstained from coming to church to hear divine service, and is a common upholder of unlawful meetings to the great disturbance and distraction of the good subjects of the kingdom contrary to the sovereign laws of our lord the king."

"What say you to this?" asked the clerk.

"I frequently attend the Church of God," Bunyan answered, "And I am, by God's grace a member with all the people over whom Christ is the head."

"You know what we mean," one judge shouted, "Do you attend the parish church of the Church of England?"

"No, I do not," Bunyan answered.

"Why not?" asked the judge.

"Because I do not find it commanded in the Word of God," Bunyan replied.

"We are commanded to pray," the judge responded.

"Yes, but not by the Common Prayer Book," Bunyan said.

"How then are we commanded to pray?" asked the judge.

"With the Spirit," Bunyan answered. Holding up his well-worn Bible, he said, "Show me the place in the Bible where the Common Prayer Book is written, or one text of Scripture that commands me to read it, and I will use it."

"We can't waste anymore time," another judge snapped. "Do you confess or not?"

"I confess," Bunyan said, "that we have many meetings together to pray to God and to exhort one another. I confess that I am guilty of nothing else."

"You will be sent back to prison until you promise to stop your preaching."

"If I were out of prison today," Bunyan said, "I would preach the gospel again tomorrow."

The judges sent him to jail. "The parting from my wife and poor children," Bunyan wrote from prison, "broke my heart to pieces."

He made leather boot straps to provide a little money for his family. Bunyan prepared himself for exile or death, but neither came. Instead, he spent year after year in jail. Other Christian prisoners came and went. He taught them from the Bible. Blest by his insights and down-to-earth explanations, they urged him to write down his meditations on the Word of God. A printer in London published them, and they encouraged Christians across England. He wrote several books, including the story of his conversion, *Grace Abounding to the Chief of Sinners*.

After twelve years behind bars, he was released. The king decided to grant nonconformist ministers permission to preach. Bunyan stopped mending pots and gave all his time to preaching, planting churches, and writing books. Before long, the king changed his mind again and banned nonconformists from preaching. But Bunyan refused to stop. Soon he landed in jail again.

During that second round in prison, he wrote a book unlike anything he had written before. Bunyan imagined the Christian life as a dangerous pilgrimage through the world to heaven. He called it, *The Pilgrim's Progress From This World to That Which is to Come*. He wrote it as an allegory, telling the story of a man named Christian

JOHN BUNYAN

"He spent year after year in jail."

who travels the difficult way to heaven, encountering trials and temptations. Throughout, he is helped by the good counsel of a man named Evangelist. Bunyan's tale was taken from his own life. He was Christian and John Gifford was Evangelist.

When he showed the story to his friend, John Owen, Owen told him to have it published. It was an instant success. Printers could not make copies fast enough. Although *The Pilgrim's Progress* made a great deal of money for printers and booksellers, Bunyan received little for it. But that did not concern him. "The true spirit of prayer," Bunyan said, "is more precious than thousands of gold and silver."

In December 1671, the king reversed course again and overturned the laws against nonconformists. Bunyan left prison for good. He became the pastor of his Bedford congregation, and he preached far and wide. "I have seen him preach to 1,200 people at seven o'clock in the morning on a working day in the middle of winter," one man recalled.

Once, a crowd of three thousand so jammed the pews and aisles of a London church to hear Bunyan preach that he had to be lifted over people to reach the pulpit. Content to serve his little flock in Bedford, he turned down offers of large salaries from churches in London.

In 1688, he died while visiting London to preach. They laid his body in Bunhill Fields, a burial ground in London for nonconformists. More than 300 years later, his books still bring comfort and inspiration to countless people. Bunyan's *Pilgrim's Progress*, translated into scores of languages, remains one of the most widely-read books in the world.

17

HUGH MACKAIL

Covenanter Martyr

(1640–1666)

In November 1666, Hugh Mackail, sick and exhausted, rode his horse across a field in the Scottish lowlands. A few days before a friend had said of him, "He would have fallen off his horse, if someone had not held him and kept him up in the saddle." Mackail, a twenty-five-year-old minister, had spent the last few weeks encouraging a band of Covenanters as they sought to protect people from the brutality of James Turner, captain of the king's dragoons. He would have stayed with the Covenanter army, but illness forced him to leave. As he weakly guided his horse forward, a company of the king's soldiers surprised him and took him prisoner to Edinburgh.

They searched Mackail for papers that might incriminate him or others, and finding none, threw him into the Tolbooth prison. He would soon be hauled before the king's council.

The council knew about Hugh Mackail. Four years earlier, Mackail had preached his last public sermon in St. Giles Kirk in Edinburgh. It was the Sunday before Covenanter ministers were to be ejected from their churches in Edinburgh by order of Parliament. The king and Parliament had forced prelacy, the rule of bishops, upon the Church of Scotland. The Scottish churches believed that the church should be governed by ruling elders and ministers chosen by the congregation—not by appointed bishops. In Mackail's sermon, he denounced government officials and bishops who persecuted faithful preachers and hurt the flock of Christ. "The Scripture often shows," he said, "that the people of God have been persecuted, sometimes by a Pharaoh on the throne, sometimes by a Haman in the state, and sometimes by a Judas in the church."

Although Mackail did not mention any government or church leaders by name, the Archbishop of St. Andrews was furious. He dispatched a party of horsemen to capture Mackail that night. But with only a moment's notice, as the horsemen searched the house, he slipped from his bed, hid in a side room and escaped. He crossed the North Sea to Holland where many Scottish refugees had fled for safety. When he returned to Scotland a few years later, the persecution raged on. Mackail joined the ejected ministers who kept in hiding, preaching to those who gathered in isolated valleys or mountainsides.

Now, as a prisoner, he stood before the king's council. Mackail admitted that he had spent some time with the armed Covenanters, but said that he had never fought with them in battle nor knew their plans. He told the council that the Covenanter forces were not rebels—but fathers trying to protect their wives and children from the cruelty of Turner's troops. The council, convinced that Mackail knew valuable information, called for the Boot to force information from him by torture. The Boot was an iron casing that wrapped around the leg and knee. A torturer placed a wedge between the knee and the metal casing and drove the wedge in with blows from a hammer, causing excruciating pain. As a guard strapped the Boot on Mackail's leg, the king's commissioner demanded him to reveal secrets of the Covenanter army. "I have told you all that I know," Mackail answered.

"Strike," the commissioner ordered. The guard firmly hit the wedge, tearing flesh and breaking bone. "Tell us what you know," the commissioner demanded after each blow.

Ten times the blows fell, shattering his knee to bits. "I protest in the sight of God," Mackail said. "I can tell you no more, though you torture every joint in my body."

When the torture ended, Hugh Mackail, unable to walk or stand on his crushed and bloodied leg, was carried away by guards who cast him into the Tolbooth prison. Friends and family petitioned the Archbishop of St. Andrews and the council for leniency but to no avail. Three weeks after his torture, Mackail was dragged before a court which found him guilty of treason and sentenced him to death. "In four days," the judge declared, "you shall be taken to the Mercat Cross of Edinburgh and hanged on a gibbet until dead. All your goods and lands are forfeited to the king."

After hearing the sentence, Mackail said in a cheerful voice, "The Lord gives life and the Lord takes away, blessed be the name of the Lord."

As guards carried him through the street to the Tolbooth prison, people wept for him. "Trust in God," Mackail told them. "Trust in God."

Back in his cell, a fellow prisoner asked, "How is your leg?"

"The fear of my neck now has made me forget my leg," Mackail answered with a smile.

He told a friend who visited him, "Good news, in four days I shall enjoy the sight of Jesus Christ!"

On the night before his execution, he wrote his final testimony. When asked what he would miss most in the world, Mackail answered, "The reading of the Scriptures."

His cousin, Doctor Matthew Mackail, stayed in his cell to encourage him and tend to his crushed leg. When Hugh awoke in the morning, he called to his fellow condemned prisoner, John Wodrow, "Get up, John! We don't look like men who are going to be hanged this day, seeing how long we stay in bed."

Mackail and Wodrow marveled at the grace of God to calm their hearts and show them His love on the day of their execution. Then Mackail prayed with his cellmate. "Now Lord, we come to your throne, where Jesus is an advocate for us. Our plea this day, is not to be free of death, nor of pain in death, but that we may witness before many people a good confession."

John Wodrow wrote his wife a final letter, "O, my heart, I thought I had known something of my dearest Lord before. But never was it so with me as since I came within the walls of this prison. He is without all comparison. O my love, love Him!"

Mackail's father came to say goodbye for the last time. They talked and prayed together. "Father," Hugh said, "My suffering will do more harm to the prelates and be more edifying to God's people, then if I continued in the ministry for twenty years."

His father, reluctant to leave, clung to his son. "Please go," Hugh told him, "but there is one more service that you can do for me. Go and pray earnestly to the Lord to be with me on the scaffold that I may be strengthened to endure to the end."

At two o'clock in the afternoon, guards carried him along the High Street to the gallows for he could not walk on his shattered leg. As he saw the people and soldiers lining the way, he said, "So is there a greater and more solemn preparation in heaven to carry my soul to Christ's bosom."

Five other Covenanters came from the Tolbooth to be executed with him. A large crowd gathered around the scaffold and hundreds more watched from windows in the buildings surrounding the Mercat Cross. As Mackail stood before the gallows, he said, "My years in the world have been few, so my words at this time will not be many."

He read from the testimony he had written the night before. Mackail affirmed his faith in Christ and his support for the National Covenants. He forgave all those responsible for his persecution, and urged everyone to repent and trust in the Lord. When he finished, he sang Psalm 31 and then prayed. Many in the crowd cried. He gave his coat to Matthew, and as he began to climb the ladder, he said in a loud voice, "I care no more to go up this ladder and over it, than if I were going home to my father's house."

As he went up, he called down to the other condemned prisoners. "Friends and fellow sufferers, do not be afraid, every step of this ladder is a step nearer to heaven."

When he stood on the top of the gallows next to the hangman he said, "This is my comfort now, that I know my Redeemer lives. I do willingly lay down my life for the truth and the cause of God, the Covenants and the work of Reformation, which were once counted the glory of this nation. And it is for endeavoring to defend this and to remove that bitter root of prelacy that I embrace this rope."

When the hangman wrapped the noose around his neck, Mackail read the final chapter of the book of Revelation and said these last words: "Farewell father and mother, friends and relations. Farewell, the world and all its delights. Farewell, meat and drink. Farewell, sun, moon, and stars. Welcome, God and father. Welcome, sweet Lord

Jesus, the mediator of the new covenant. Welcome, blessed Spirit of grace, God of all consolation. Welcome, Glory. Welcome, eternal life. Welcome, death."

Matthew Mackail stood below the gallows to perform one last act of kindness for his cousin. The body of a hanged man would often writhe in pain for several minutes before death came. When Hugh Mackail dropped, Matthew clung to his legs and helped him to a swifter and less painful death. For years after, Matthew wore Hugh's black coat until it fell apart in honor of his martyred cousin.

18

DONALD CARGILL

"He Spoke Like No Other"

(c. 1610–1681)

In January 1680, two Covenanters, Donald Cargill and Henry Hall, dined at an inn in Queensferry. They had been on the run for years. King Charles II and his government officials in Scotland sought their lives for resisting the king's oppression of the Church of Scotland. Years earlier, in order to win Scottish support for his claim to the throne, Charles II had signed the National Covenant and the Solemn League and Covenant, promising the Scots not to interfere with the church. He told the Scottish people then, "that if in any time coming, you hear or see me breaking that Covenant, you must tell me of it and remind me of my oath."

With Scottish help, Charles II was crowned king of Britain in 1660. Immediately, he broke his promises to the Scots. He took steps to abolish Presbyterian church government in Scotland and replace it with prelacy, the rule of bishops—bishops of his choosing. Scottish ministers like Donald Cargill or Scottish nobles like Henry Hall who resisted the king's control of the church lost their homes and were declared outlaws. Cargill went into hiding, ministering to people in the hills and fields across the land.

On the day that Cargill and Hall ate dinner in Queensferry, the governor got word of their presence. He went to arrest them. Hall and Cargill fought back. Hall received a fatal blow to the head. Cargill, although wounded, narrowly escaped.

A Christian woman found Cargill, weak and bleeding. She got him to a doctor who dressed the wound. After sleeping that night in a barn, he slipped away to preach. His wound still bleeding, he spoke to a crowd gathered on a hillside. They hung on every word. When he finished preaching, he sat down exhausted. "I think preaching and praying go best with you," a man told him, "when you are in the greatest danger."

"Yes," said Cargill, "I believe it is so. The more my enemies thrust at me the more I sense the Lord has helped me." And then he quoted a verse from Psalm 118: "The Lord is my strength and song and has become my salvation."

From childhood, Cargill had a deep faith in Christ; although, as a young man, he wrestled with doubts and depression. One day, his mental anguish overwhelmed him, and he decided to take his own life. Early in the morning, he walked to the edge of a deep coal pit with the intention of throwing himself into it. But as he stood there, the voice of the Lord came into his mind, "Son, be of good cheer, your sins are forgiven."

Cargill left the precipice filled with peace. He was never again tempted to do himself harm, but rather strove to do others good.

After Cargill completed his degree in philosophy at St. Andrews University, his father urged him to become a minister. But he refused saying, "The work of the ministry is too great a burden for my weak shoulders."

His father kept pressing him and praying that his son would change his mind. So Cargill set aside time for prayer and fasting about his future. He read a verse in the third chapter of Ezekiel: "Son of man, eat what is before you, eat this scroll; then go and speak to the house of Israel." These words made such a strong impression on him that Cargill dedicated himself to the ministry from that day forward. Eventually, he became the pastor of a church in Glasgow, serving there for seven years before he was banished for refusing to acknowledge the king as the head of the church.

A few months after Charles II became king of Britain, all the churches of England and Scotland were called to commemorate his coming to the throne. In the short time that Charles II had ruled, he showed himself to be a dishonest and immoral despot. On the day appointed for the commemoration of the king, a large throng of people came to Cargill's church to hear him preach. They thought that he would speak about the blessings of Charles II's new reign. But when Cargill entered the pulpit he said, "We thought once to bless the day wherein the king came home again, but now we think we shall have reason to curse it. Whoever of the Lord's people this day are rejoicing, their joy will soon be turned to mourning. The king will be the most woeful sight that ever the poor Church of Scotland saw. Woe, woe unto him, his name shall stink while the world stands, for treachery, tyranny, and lechery!"

Cargill's words enraged the authorities, and they sought to imprison him. So he began his life on the run, sometimes living in caves, or cottages of friends, or out in the moors. He preached wherever he could. For years, Donald Cargill avoided the king's men, sojourning throughout Scotland preaching and baptizing and encouraging all in the Lord. Cargill had no family of his own. His family became the poor hill folk who risked their lives to hear him preach.

"He spoke like no other," one man said who often traveled far to hear Cargill, "for his words went right through you."

Cargill showed his hearers the blackness of their own hearts. "Those who know themselves best," he said, "will fear themselves most." But then he pointed them to Jesus Christ, urging all to put their faith in Him. "Dwell in the clefts of the Rock of Christ," he pleaded, "hide yourself in the wounds of Christ, wrap yourself in his promises."

The people longed to hear faithful preaching, often walking great distances to hear the Word of God. Cargill's sermons were often shorter than most Covenanter preachers, and his hearers wished he would preach longer. Someone asked him why his sermons and his prayers were short, saying, "Sir, it is long between meals, and we are starving; all is good, sweet, and wholesome that you deliver. Why don't you give us more?"

"I never try to preach or pray with my own gifts," Cargill answered. "When my heart is not affected, I always think it's time to quit. What comes not from the heart, I have little hope that it will go to the hearts of others."

He never stayed long in one place, living on the run. Yet he managed to give to the poor out of his poverty and always had a word of grace for the discouraged.

Many times he barely avoided capture. Once when soldiers had chased him for miles, he rushed down a steep hillside and leaped across a narrow but deep chasm. The pursuing soldiers dared not jump it, and Cargill escaped. Later a friend told him, "You made a good leap."

"Yes," Cargill replied, "but I had a good running start."

One day a large crowd gathered at Loudoun Hill near Newmilns in western Scotland where Cargill preached a sermon and baptized some children. When the service ended, the people pressed him to preach to them again. He agreed and began to teach. But soldiers in Glasgow had got word of the meeting. They rushed on horseback to the spot.

The soldiers caught Cargill and his congregation by surprise. They scattered into a nearby thicket and threw themselves facedown in the heather. The soldiers opened fire into the brush, but by God's grace no one was killed or captured that day.

As the king's officials and soldiers grew more violent, Cargill grew more resistant, urging the people to remain true to their faith and defend themselves against the assaults of the dragoons. One Sunday in September 1680, at a large conventicle not far from Stirling, he made a bold, and perhaps a rash, step. Cargill took it upon himself to excommunicate King Charles II and several of the Scottish nobles who led the persecution of the Covenanters from the council in Edinburgh.

When word of Cargill's actions got back to the king's advisors, they exploded with rage. The Bishop of Edinburgh called Cargill "demented and mad" and his actions "treasonable and sacrilegious."

The next Lord's Day, Cargill told a crowd gathered in a remote spot, "I know I will be condemned by many for excommunicating those wicked men. But I know I am approved of by God, and I am persuaded that what I have done on earth is ratified in heaven."

In 1681, after nearly twenty years of ministering as a hunted man, the king's soldiers captured Cargill and brought him to trial in Edinburgh. One member of the council who stood in judgment over him was a college friend of Cargill's, the Duke of Rothes. Rothes had signed the Solemn League and Covenant with Cargill when they were students at St. Andrews University. But Rothes turned his back on the Covenanters and became one of their fiercest persecutors. However, Rothes's wife had remained a strong supporter of Covenanter preachers. Rothes was one of the men Cargill had excommunicated along with the king a few months before.

As Cargill stood before the king's council, Rothes angrily denounced him and threatened him with torture and death. "My Lord Rothes," Cargill said, "stop threatening me. Die what death I will, your eyes shall not see it."

This came to pass—Rothes died a few days later. The night before Rothes died, he asked his wife to call for one of her ministers to talk with him. "My own ministers are good to live with but not to die with," he said.

"We all thought little of what Cargill did in excommunicating us," Rothes said to a friend from his deathbed, "but I find that sentence binding upon me now, and it will bind me to eternity."

After Rothes's death, a member of the council said, "We banish these men from us, and yet when dying, we call for them. This is melancholy work!"

While Cargill awaited his fate in prison, a Christian woman came to visit him. With tears in her eyes she said, "These heaven-daring enemies are planning the most violent death for you."

"Do not be troubled," Cargill told her, "for all that they can do to me, will be to hang me up, cut me down, and chop off my old head, and then farewell to them. They will be done with me and I with them forever."

The council condemned him to death by hanging for high treason. The sentence was pronounced by the sound of the trumpet. "That is a weary sound," Cargill said, "but the sound of the last trumpet will be a joyful sound to me and all that will be found having Christ's righteousness."

When the day of execution arrived, guards led Cargill—his Bible in hand—to the scaffold next to the Mercat Cross of Edinburgh. An enormous crowd looked on. Cargill quoted some lines from Psalm 118 and began to preach to the spectators, but the beating drums of a company of soldiers muffled his words. Cargill smiled and said to the people, "You see we have no liberty to speak what we wanted, but God knows our hearts."

Each time that Cargill tried to speak, the drums drowned him out. But the crowd heard him say, "Now, I am as sure of my interest in Christ, and peace with God, as all within this Bible and the Spirit of God can make me. This is the sweetest and most glorious day that ever my eyes did see."

As he climbed the ladder to the scaffold, Cargill called out, "The Lord knows I go up this ladder with less fear than ever I entered the pulpit to preach."

When he reached the top, he said, "I bless the Lord, and I forgive all men the wrongs they have done to me."

Before the hangman did his work, Cargill said, "Farewell friends in Christ; farewell acquaintances and earthly enjoyments; farewell reading and preaching, praying and believing, wanderings, reproach, and sufferings! Welcome Father, Son, and Holy Spirit; into thy hands I commit my spirit!"

19

RICHARD BAXTER

"A Pen in God's Hand"

(1615–1691)

In 1640, the people of Kidderminster were fed up with their minister who spent more time in the alehouse getting drunk than he did in church. He collected his pay, but only preached a few shoddy sermons a year and hired an assistant to do the rest of the work. But that man was a lazy drunkard too. The congregation couldn't fire him since only the bishop could remove a minister from his charge. When the Puritan-majority Parliament took control of reforming the Church of England over the objections of King Charles I, the people of Kidderminster finally received permission to call a new preacher.

A young, tall and thin minister named Richard Baxter took the post. Baxter loved Jesus Christ and he wanted the people of Kidderminster, England, to love Him too. The church building was large, but services were poorly attended. A few townspeople had a living faith in Christ, but most had no spiritual interest. "They did not read the Scriptures or any good book," Baxter said. "Few of them could read at all, or had a Bible. They never prayed in their families. They could be divided into two groups—those that lived quietly and did their work and the rest were drunkards."

Many of the townspeople misunderstood Baxter's preaching, disliked his Puritan views, and despised his call for holy living. Not
long after he arrived in Kidderminster, civil war broke out between
King Charles I and Parliament. Those who disliked Baxter's ministry
called him an enemy of the king. One day an official saw Baxter on the
street and shouted, "There goes a traitor!" Richard Baxter's friends
urged him to leave the city for a time for his own safety. So Baxter
traveled for several months with the parliamentary army, preaching
to the troops until he grew so ill he had to withdraw. When Parliament defeated King Charles, and the Puritan leader Oliver Cromwell
ruled the land as Lord Protector, Baxter returned to Kidderminster.

Delighted to be back, Baxter gave his all to win the townspeople to
Christ. He labored to preach the good news of Jesus Christ as simply
and earnestly as he could. "I preach," Baxter said, "as a dying man
to dying men."

He visited the townspeople house by house, encouraging them
to follow Christ, answering their questions about his sermons and
praying for their needs. Many crowded into his home on Thursday
evenings to hear God's Word, sing, and pray.

Since Kidderminster had no doctor, Baxter read books on medicine. He treated the sick and gave out medicines, never charging
anyone a penny. Baxter was unmarried then, and he thought of the
people as his own children. He used his money to help them. On
his small salary and the money he made from the sale of the books
he wrote, Baxter gave generously to the poor. If a poor family had
no Bible, he bought them one. He sent the brightest and hardest-
working students from the Kidderminster school to college where
he and some of his friends paid their way.

Soon people filled the large church to overflowing. Church officers built five wooden galleries to handle the crowds that came to
worship and hear the Word of God. Many people put their trust in
Christ, and lives were transformed. Once a week the young people
met in a large group for a three-hour prayer meeting. Clusters of
families throughout the town gathered on Saturday nights to talk
about the sermons, read the Bible, and pray for God's blessing on
the coming Lord's Day.

"When I first arrived," Baxter wrote, "just one family in a hundred
worshiped God in their homes. Many were drunk and disorderly in

the streets on the Lord's Day. Later, you might hear a hundred families singing psalms and repeating sermons as you passed by their houses."

Word spread throughout England of the awakening of faith in Kidderminster. When Baxter preached in other towns, the poor and downtrodden packed the churches and crowded around the open doors and windows to hear him.

"I praise my dear Redeemer," Baxter wrote, "who blessed my labors with such encouraging success. O, what am I, a worthless worm, that God should so abundantly encourage me when godly ministers labored fifty years in one place and scarcely saw one or two people converted!"

Baxter performed his many labors while struggling with serious illness. Nearly all of his life he suffered from intestinal troubles, severe pain, and tuberculosis. Once after three months of wracking pain in his head and body, Baxter wrote, "God has so much increased my languishing that I had reason to think that my time on earth would not be long. If my flesh and heart should fail, God is the rock of my heart and my portion forever."

Throughout his fifty years of ministry, Baxter wrote books—nearly 150 books, more than any other Puritan writer of his day. He wrote technical works on theology for scholars and devotional books for all believers. His book, *The Reformed Pastor*, is a classic guide to ministers on how to care for Christ's flock. His most loved work is *The Saint's Everlasting Rest*, a book about heaven. He wrote it while he was in the midst of a grave sickness that almost took his life. He wanted to help Christians prepare for eternal life by pointing their thoughts toward heaven. The glories of Jesus Christ and life in heaven became the great themes of his writing and preaching. God used *The Saint's Everlasting Rest* to lead countless people to faith in Christ. One Puritan minister who was converted after reading it wrote, "It is a book that scarce can be overvalued and for which I have cause forever to bless God."

Although Richard Baxter enjoyed freedom from persecution during the years when Cromwell ruled, he supported the restoration of the monarchy. In 1660, when King Charles II was crowned in London, the king made promises to Christian ministers in England that the Scriptures would guide his reign. But like his father before him, he wanted to control the church in Britain. At first, Charles II did not have the political strength to impose his will. He tried to win the favor of influential ministers. Charles offered to make Baxter the Bishop of Hereford, but Baxter, fearing that he would be expected to compromise his principles, declined.

After two years, when Charles had consolidated his power, his government passed the Act of Uniformity. It demanded that all ministers take an oath consenting to everything contained in the Book of Common Prayer and promising to never attempt to reform the church. Baxter and more than two thousand other ministers in the Church of England refused to take such an unbiblical oath. They were branded "nonconformists" and thrown out of their churches, losing their livings and their homes. The government forbade them from preaching under pain of fines or imprisonment. "We sit in unprofitable silence or in prison," Baxter wrote, "and are considered as the scum of the earth."

He eventually moved to London to write books and preach occasionally in meetinghouses. But the authorities refused to leave Baxter alone. Church leaders placed spies in the audience wherever Baxter spoke. "I scarcely preached a sermon," Baxter wrote, "or said a prayer to God without someone being tempted to accuse me of some heinous crime."

For twenty-five years, Baxter faced harassment and fines. Several times he was imprisoned—sometimes for a few days, sometimes for many months. Once, after preaching a sermon at a meetinghouse, he returned home and went straight to bed in extreme pain. Soon constables burst into his house, waving a warrant to arrest him and seize his property. They carried Baxter to jail. "They took my books and my goods," Baxter recorded, "even the bed that I lay sick on, and sold them all." Then he added, "O how little our wrathful enemies can do against us, in comparison of what our sin and the justice of God can do!"

In 1685, during the short and disastrous reign of King James II, the persecution of nonconformists intensified. Agents of the king seized seventy-year-old Richard Baxter and delivered him to Westminster Hall in London to stand in the dock before the chief justice. Baxter was charged with sedition for criticizing the rule of bishops in his books. He denied the charges, but when he asked for time to mount a defense of his writings, the chief justice said, "I will not give him another minute to save his life. He is one of the greatest rogues and rascals in the kingdom."

As the trial progressed, the chief justice stopped Baxter from speaking in his own defense. "He's poisoned the world with his Kidderminster doctrine—the hypocritical villain!" the judge declared.

His attorney pled with the judge that Baxter was loyal to the king and the nation, "I beseech your Lordship, suffer me a word for my client. It is well known to all intelligent men in this nation that Mr. Baxter supported the restoration of King Charles II. King Charles would have made him a bishop if he had conformed to the Act of Uniformity."

"Aye," said the judge, "we know that, but what ailed the old blockhead, the unthankful villain that he would not conform?" The judge grew red in the face and shouted, "He's a conceited, stubborn, fanatical dog. Hang him; he deserves to be whipped through the city."

When Baxter tried to speak again, the judge cried out, "Richard, Richard, do you think we'll hear you poison the court? Richard, you old knave; you have written books enough to load a cart and every one is full of sedition and treason."

"My Lord," Baxter replied, "I think I can clearly answer all that is laid to my charge, and I shall do it briefly."

But the judge refused to allow him to speak. The chief justice summed up the case for the jury: "It is notoriously known that there's been a design to ruin the king and the nation," he said. Then, pointing to Baxter, he added, "And this person has been the main firebrand."

He told the jury that there was no doubt that Baxter's writings were full of treason, and so they must find him guilty. The jury grouped together for a few minutes and immediately declared him guilty. The court ordered Baxter to pay a huge fine, and condemned him to prison until he paid it in full or died. The chief justice had wanted Baxter publicly whipped through the streets of London, but others intervened and prevented it.

Guards cast Richard Baxter into prison. Many friends and fellow ministers visited him. All who came reported that he was in good spirits, full of the joy of the Lord. "Prepare for trials," he told them, "and the best preparation for them is a life of faith and self-denial."

After nearly two years, the government commuted Baxter's sentence and released him from prison. Although his body was failing and he lacked the strength to go out and preach, he opened his home to all who would come. In the morning and in the evening he read the Bible and preached to them. And he continued writing books.

In his old age, Baxter expressed regrets for the emphasis he placed on certain aspects of the Christian life as a young man. "In my younger years," he said, "my main concern was my actual failings. But now I'm much more troubled about my lack of a greater love to God and not thinking enough about and longing for the life to come with God in heaven."

As a young minister Baxter didn't think sermons on the attributes of God or the joys of heaven were as important as other things. "Now," Baxter wrote, "I would rather read, hear, and meditate on God in heaven than on any other subject."

He told those who visited him as he neared death, "Be mindful of the shortness of time, the greatness of God, and the riches of the grace of Christ."

He advised people to meditate on heaven, especially the description of heaven found in Hebrews chapter 12. "That Scripture," Baxter said, "deserved a thousand thousand thoughts."

During his last days, a friend tried to comfort him, saying, "Remember how many have been blessed through your preaching and writing."

"I was but a pen in God's hands," Baxter replied, "and what praise is due to a pen?"

20

JOSEPH ALLEINE

A Good Head and a Better Heart

(1634–1668)

In 1645, the Alleine family gathered to mourn the loss of Edward, their son and brother. Edward died young. He had completed his university training and made a good start as a minister of the gospel. His death was a stiff blow to his family. In the midst of their grief, Edward's younger brother, twelve-year-old Joseph, approached Mr. Alleine. "Father," he said, "I would like to follow in Edward's steps and serve God as a minister. Could I begin now to prepare?"

This was music to his father's ears. Taking his son in his arms, he said that he would make plans at once. His father attached him to a competent schoolmaster and for the next four years, Joseph poured his heart and strength into the study of Greek, Latin, mathematics, and logic. By the age of sixteen he was admitted to Oxford University. His diligence in pursuing Christ at college became well known. He rose before four o'clock every morning to spend time alone with God. "Come now," he would tell his friends each morning, "let this day be spent for God. Let us live this day well."

Alleine's face lit up whenever conversation turned to God. Sometimes, when speaking about the love of God, he would break off and say, "I am full of the mercies of the Lord! O praise the Lord with me; O help me to praise the Lord!"

"He always had such a great love for praying," one classmate noted, "that he and his friends could hardly ever walk and talk together, before Joseph would say, 'Come, we must pray together right now.' His prayers were taken up more with praising and admiring Jesus Christ than asking for his own needs."

In 1655, Joseph Alleine became the assistant pastor of St. Mary Magdalene Church in Taunton, England. George Newton, the senior pastor, immediately saw his love for the Lord. "He had a good head and a better heart," Newton said. "His conversation with others was always mingled with heavenly talk."

Alleine poured his energies into serving his flock. He spent six hours every weekday afternoon and evening visiting families in their homes. "I bless God for the fruit of these visits," he said, "God has used me in these as an instrument of good for souls."

When Alleine stood in the pulpit, his tall, erect frame looked imposing, but his cheerful countenance drew people into his message. He strove to set before his hearers the grace of God in Jesus Christ. "Never think you can convert yourself," he said. "It is a resurrection from the dead, a new creation, and a work of absolute omnipotence. Are not these out of the reach of human power? This is a supernatural work. You must cry, 'Grace! Grace!' What but free grace could move God to love you?"

There was a great sense of urgency about Alleine. "He lived," one friend said, "as one that seriously believed that he must quickly be in the heavenly church and live with God in Christ for ever!" He loved Christ and longed for heaven, and he wanted everyone to join him there. "O what a shout there will be when Christ shall come in his glory!" he preached, "I hope all here present shall contribute to that shout. I hope to pass an eternity with you in the praises of our God."

Richard Baxter, the famous Puritan pastor, admired Alleine's preaching. "He had great skill in the public explanation and application of the Scriptures," Baxter observed, "so melting, so convincing, so powerful!"

"He was full of holy projects," Pastor Newton said, "often thinking of ways to more effectively promote the honor of Christ and the benefits of souls."

Many in the town came to a living faith in Christ through Alleine's preaching and his home visits. He loved his congregation and they loved him. "We saw in his face," one parishioner said, "how very dear we were to him."

When the Act of Uniformity became law in 1662, forcing all ministers to conform to the king's demands for worship, Alleine wrestled with what to do. Should he conform and keep preaching or refuse and lose his fruitful ministry? "Before the Act of Uniformity came forth," his wife said, "my husband was very earnest day and night asking God to make his way plain."

"I will not leave the work of saving souls," he said, "for small and dubious matters." But in the end he could not in good conscience conform to the government's demands for worship. Agents of the bishop expelled him from his charge. But he refused to stop ministering to his people even though he was barred from preaching in church. "He resolved," his wife said, "to go on with his work in private—preaching in our home and visiting from house to house—until he should be carried to prison or banished."

The bishops filled the pulpits of the expelled pastors with incompetent and unspiritual men. Alleine worried about his flock. "Now they have fallen into the hands of such ministers who have neither the skill nor will to save souls," he lamented.

Whenever word spread to the Taunton congregation of a secret preaching meeting—whether by day or by night—they crowded into homes and barns to hear Alleine preach. "This was a great encouragement to my husband," his wife reported, "and he went on with much vigor and affection in his work, both in preaching and visiting from house to house."

Alleine also preached to the people in the outlying villages where their ministers had been ejected. Although he was often threatened and nearly caught on several occasions, the Lord protected him from the hands of his pursuers. "If it please the Lord to grant me three months liberty to do some work before I go to prison," he said, "I should count myself favored by God and should go with more cheerfulness."

He spent himself crowding in as much ministry as he could while he had the opportunity—often preaching twice each day and visiting three or four homes. Then after nine months of feverish activity, an officer arrested him and brought him before a judge. "You have broken the Act of Uniformity by your preaching," the judge declared.

"Your honor," Alleine replied, "I have not violated the act for I never preached in any church or chapel or any place of public worship since I was ejected from my pulpit. I only preached to my own family and to others that came to hear me."

Despite the lack of evidence against him, the judge ordered him to report to prison the following day. "I thank God," Alleine said, "for what He has done in these past months, I am going to prison full of joy, confident that all these things will turn out to the furtherance of the gospel and the glory of God."

Because he was free for one more night, he sent word to his congregation to come and meet him after midnight. Hundreds arrived in the dark to hear their beloved pastor preach one more time. For three hours he preached and prayed. The next morning when he started to leave Taunton for jail, a great crowd came to say farewell. "The streets were lined on all sides with people," an eyewitness said. "Many followed him on foot some miles out of town with such weeping that he could scarcely bear it. But the Lord so strengthened him that he was able to encourage them by his cheerful countenance and expressions."

"He went to prison," his wife said, "not only contented, but joyful to suffer for the name of Jesus and his gospel."

When friends complained to him about his persecutors, Alleine said, "My only wish for them is that they might be thoroughly converted and sanctified and saved in the day of the Lord Jesus."

Many people gathered outside the barred windows of his cell to hear Alleine preach the Word of God. He wrote many letters of encouragement to his flock and other friends around the kingdom from prison. "My desire is for our friends to help us in our praises," he wrote. "Our tongues are too little to speak forth the goodness and grace of God—help us in our praises."

In May 1664—after a year in prison—Joseph Alleine was released. He promptly resumed preaching in homes. A year later, he was arrested and hauled to court again. The justices accused him of leading "riotous assemblies." When Alleine tried to explain that the gatherings were quiet meetings for preaching and prayer, the justices interrupted him with scorn. "You rogue," one man in the court shouted, "you deserve to be hanged!"

They found him guilty, levied a heavy fine against him, and sent him back to prison.

Those who observed Joseph Alleine's sufferings both inside and outside of prison marveled that he never spoke a word of complaint, but rather he thanked God for all His mercies. One of his fellow prisoners said of Alleine's Christ-centered thoughts, "He could be in jail and in heaven at once!"

The stark and unhealthy conditions of prison took a toll on Alleine's body. When free, he wore himself out with his labors, preaching and counseling through the day and night, never getting enough sleep. Not long after he was released from his second prison term, his health broke down. It got so that he could not move his arms. Looking at his useless limbs, he smiled and said, "The Lord has given and the Lord has taken away. Blessed be the name of the Lord."

Even on his deathbed, visitors reported that he was continually pouring out praises and thanksgivings to God. He died saying, "My life is hid with Christ in God."

After his death at the age of thirty-four, many of Joseph Alleine's writings were published. His *An Alarm to the Unconverted* became a Puritan classic. In it, he calls sinners to put their trust in Christ alone for salvation and not in their own good works. He wrote that those who come to Christ must receive him as their Savior from sin and as their Lord whose commandments they must obey. Throughout the centuries, many souls have turned to Christ through Alleine's writings, and they proved to be an inspiration for the great evangelists—John Wesley, George Whitefield, and Charles Spurgeon.

21

PHILIP HENRY

"Heavenly Henry"

(1631–1691)

Philip Henry, an English boy in his early teens, knelt in prayer. For several days he had been examining his heart and found it black and full of sin. From his earliest days, his mother had urged him to trust in Christ for the forgiveness of his sins. Often during the week, she brought her bright son to hear the finest preachers in London. Every Sunday they attended the morning and evening services at their home church, St. Margaret's Church, Westminster. She arranged for Philip to hear morning lectures presented by the renowned ministers who were writing *The Westminster Confession of Faith*. At age twelve, he began to take notes of every lecture and sermon he heard. He kept them in a file and reviewed them—a practice he continued all his life.

Philip's family was not wealthy. However, his father served King Charles I as the keeper of his orchards at Whitehall in London, and so the family enjoyed certain privileges. Among Philip's childhood playmates were Prince Charles, the heir to the throne, and his brother Prince James. Philip attended Westminster School, one of the finest schools in the kingdom.

His mother had recently died. On her sickbed she had told Philip, "My head is in heaven, and my heart is in heaven; it is just one more step and I shall be there too."

Now his mother's influence and all the Christian messages were bearing fruit. He realized that without Christ, he was utterly lost. "I confessed my sins before God," Philip said, "and received Jesus Christ as my Lord and Righteousness. I devoted and dedicated my whole life, absolutely and unreservedly, to His service. Bless the Lord O my soul!"

He remained true to his pledge to dedicate his life to God's service. He went to Christ Church College in Oxford to train for the ministry. Not long after arriving at Oxford, he wrote a personal pledge: "I do unreservedly take God in Christ to be mine; and give myself to Him, to be His, to love Him, to fear Him, to serve and obey Him. I do renounce all my sins with hearty sorrow and cast myself only upon free grace, through the merits of Christ, for pardon and forgiveness. I propose, God enabling me, to walk in godliness as much as I can with delight and cheerfulness, knowing that my labor shall not be in vain in the Lord."

While Henry attended university, the English Civil War ended when the armies of Parliament defeated the forces of King Charles I. They took the king prisoner. In the winter of 1648–49, Henry was on leave from college, visiting his father in London. A huge scaffold was built outside the gate of Whitehall where his father worked. On January 30, 1649, Henry stood before the scaffold, among a throng of thousands, to witness the beheading of the king. When the blow of the ax fell, a great groan went up from the people, and then soldiers on horseback dispersed the crowd. Philip Henry left the scene heartsick. Although he believed Charles had abused his powers, he ever after said, "The execution of the king was wholly unjustified and a national sin."

Philip Henry dedicated himself to his studies, viewing it all as preparation for serving God. He met with other Christian students for Bible study and prayer. He enjoyed the preaching of the great Puritan theologians, John Owen and Thomas Goodwin, carefully taking notes of every sermon.

Henry won honors at Oxford University for his papers and his public speaking. When he was not preparing for essays or exams, he spent his time searching the Scriptures, and collecting helpful insights on Bible passages. "I read other books," he said, "that I may be better able to understand the Scripture."

He graduated in December, 1652. A month later, he preached his first sermon. He wrote, "May the Lord make use of me as an instrument of His glory and His Church's good in this high and holy calling."

Philip Henry became the minister of the church in Worthenbury, a village in the heart of the English countryside. His life stood in stark contrast to the lives of the members of his congregation. He grew up in London, near the court of the king, educated in the finest schools. Most of them had spent their lives as poor tenant farmers in a small village with little formal education. Few people in Worthenbury came to church. One local woman said, "On the Lord's Day, most people spend their time in the alehouse or playing ball."

When Henry arrived in Worthenbury he wrote in his diary, "Lord, give me souls." The people of the town quickly discovered that their new minister loved Christ and loved the Bible and loved them. "O make Christ your all!" he urged them. "How sweet it is to a lost undone sinner to be acquainted with a Savior!"

Though highly educated and eloquent, Henry did not preach over their heads. His messages were clear and earnest. "He spoke to their hearts with charming and pleasing power," wrote one who knew him well.

He loved to read God's Word in church, in family devotions, and in private. "Bless God," he often said, "for every book and every chapter and every line in the Bible."

Philip Henry's life in the church and at home revolved around prayer. He warned against cold and formal prayers. "When we pray," Henry said, "we should fill our hearts with love to God, look up to the Spirit and hold fast to His sweet promises." Henry taught believers to work at developing a heavenly frame of mind before beginning prayer. "We must stir up our affections, and labor with our hearts," he said. But he solemnly warned against praying "in our own strength without an eye to the Spirit."

Although Henry was spiritually minded, he did not neglect the physical needs of the people. If he heard that someone was sick, he made straight for his door. He sat at the bedsides of the ill, bringing words of encouragement and prayer. "I aimed," Henry said, "not only to do the sick person good, but to bless their friends and family in the house."

He gave generously to the needy, setting aside 10% of his income to give to the poor. "He is no fool," Henry said, "who parts with that which he cannot keep, when he is sure to gain that which he cannot lose."

Henry strove through the grace of God to be kind and to think the best of others. He made it his rule never to speak of anyone's faults. Many of his friends said that they had never heard him speak evil of anybody. When he overheard negative talk about people behind their backs, he reminded the speaker, "Remember Leviticus 19:14: 'Thou shalt not curse the deaf.'"

Soon Henry's preaching and praying, his kindness and generosity made an impression. People who hadn't darkened the door of the church in years began to attend services. He spent a good part of each week visiting people house by house. Henry taught them from the Bible, instructed the children in the faith and prayed for their needs. Many came to him for spiritual counseling. A growing number of people put their trust in Jesus Christ. The church filled with worshipers.

He challenged new believers to make time each day to read and meditate on the Word of God. "When you know what God wants you to do," he told them, "resolve to do it. But you will say, 'I cannot.' I know you cannot, but Jesus Christ will help you. If you come to Him daily, knowing your own impotency, He will strengthen you by His Spirit. He will plant grace, water it, and make it grow and bring forth fruit."

Philip Henry came to Worthenbury a single man, but before long, he fell in love with a young woman who lived nearby named Katherine Matthews. Her father was a wealthy country gentleman who, at first, refused to allow Henry to court his daughter because he did not want his only child to marry a poor minister. Henry was persistent, and eventually gained his permission. Katherine's friends couldn't understand her interest in Henry. "Although he is a fine preacher," one told her, "he is a stranger to our region. We do not even know where he came from."

"True," Katherine replied, "but I know where he is going, and I would like to go with him."

They married in the spring of 1659. He called her "dear heart," and always referred to their wedding day as "a day of mercy never to be forgotten." Within the first eight years of their marriage, they had six children, two sons, John and Matthew, and four daughters. All who visited the Henry home were struck by the strong bond of Christian love and joy between Philip and Katherine and their children. Tragedy struck when their son John died of measles at age 6. Matthew and the girls survived. Matthew Henry became a minister and wrote a commentary on the whole Bible that became the most widely used commentary in the English-speaking world.

On their twentieth wedding anniversary, Philip Henry wrote in his diary, "We have been married for twenty years and we've received more than 20,000 mercies from the Lord: to God be the glory."

Although a man of strong convictions, Philip Henry mourned the divisions that fractured Christ's church and separated believers from one another. He organized an association of pastors in the area where Episcopalian, Presbyterian, and Independent ministers gathered for prayer and mutual encouragement. Henry's warmth and wisdom won the hearts of the neighboring ministers. They sought him out for advice and comfort.

His reputation for gospel preaching and his warm personal faith spread throughout England. People began to refer to him as "Heavenly Henry." Churches in larger cities asked him to be their minister, including a church in London which offered him a much greater salary. Philip Henry declined them all, content to serve the Lord where he was. "He did not seek great things for himself," his son said.

After the death of Cromwell, Philip Henry supported the restoration of the monarchy. He rejoiced when his childhood playmate, Prince Charles, returned from exile and was crowned King Charles II. This joy was short lived. Soon persecution came as Charles II, like his father before him, tried to force all ministers to conform to the king's control of the church. Henry foresaw the great difficulties to come and prayed, "Lord prepare your people for the fiery trial."

King Charles II insisted that all ministers in the land use the new Book of Common Prayer in their worship services. In the fall of 1600 and the spring of 1661, Henry was hauled before a court for not reading from the worship book, although it was not yet required by law. Despite the threats of the authorities, he continued to lead worship as he believed God had directed in the Bible. The government confiscated his pay. "I cannot sin against my conscience," Henry said. "I shall choose rather to lose all."

The pressure grew. Across the kingdom, ministers who would not conform to the king's demands were fined and jailed. "A time of trouble in the nation," Henry wrote in his diary in January 1661, "many good men imprisoned. I am yet in peace, blessed be God, but I expect suffering. Lord, prepare me for it!"

In 1662, the Act of Uniformity became law. It declared that any minister who refused to pledge complete acceptance of the liturgy, doctrines and government of the Church of England was to be cast out of his church. Philip Henry wrestled with whether he should conform to the requirements of the act. He hated divisions and treasured the peace of the church. Henry counseled with his fellow ministers and prayed. A church official urged him to conform. "You will lose your living," he said. "You are a young man, and are you wiser than the king and bishops?"

In the end, Henry refused to take the required oath. The act declared that all who did not take the oath were presumed dead and their pulpits would be filled by other ministers. The law took effect on August 24, 1662, Philip Henry's thirty-first birthday. He wrote in his diary, "This is the day of the year on which I was born, and also the day of the year on which, by law, I died! This is the saddest day for England since the death of Edward VI, but even this is for good."

Philip Henry was ejected from his church, as were 2,000 other nonconformists ministers. He gave up his home in Worthenbury, and moved to Broad Oak, the country estate that his wife inherited when her father died. The Henrys used it to provide for other ministers who were removed from their churches and lived in poverty.

Unlike many other nonconformists, Philip Henry happily worshiped at his local Church of England congregation. He would not judge the motives of ministers who conformed to the king's demands. "By my goodwill," Henry said, "I seek the public peace of the church."

Many of the sermons he and his family heard were poor. But he always sought to make the best of it. "It is a mercy, we have bread," he told his family, "though it is not of the finest wheat." When someone criticized a preacher's message, Henry often replied, "There's nothing perfect under the sun."

One Sunday morning a visiting minister preached a sermon full of bitter accusations against nonconformists. Philip Henry's friends and family wondered if he would go and hear him again in the evening service. Henry went saying, "If he does not know his duty, I know mine. I bless God. I can find honey in a carcass."

Philip Henry was not permitted to preach or administer the sacraments publicly. He could teach in his own house, and so on Sunday afternoons, friends and family crowded into the Henry home to hear him preach and pray. A number of people turned to Christ through his teaching and preaching after he was cast out of the church.

For most of the next twenty years, the authorities harassed Philip Henry for his religious convictions. On several occasions he was brought before a judge and fined. Twice he was imprisoned for short periods of time. A judge commanded him to appear before his court for baptizing one of his own children. When he went to London to help friends suffering during the plague, officials accused him of violating the law. Vicious rumors were spread about him. One judge told him, "By the grace of God, I will root you out of the country."

Henry never lost hope in God's care. His study of church history encouraged him. "I find afflictions and persecutions have been always the lot of the people of God," he said, "but God has still upheld His church, and will do it to the end."

When Charles II died in 1685, his brother James became king, and he increased the persecution of nonconformist ministers. Once when Henry protested a large fine levied by a court upon him for supposedly preaching illegally, a judge issued a warrant for the confiscation of some of Henry's property. Constables burst onto his estate and proceeded to haul away thirty-three cart-loads of goods. A cry of protest arose in the surrounding countryside over the ill treatment that Philip Henry endured. "He bore it," his son said, "with his usual serenity of mind, not at all disturbed by it."

"Alas, this is nothing compared to what others suffer," Henry told his family.

In 1688, a revolution swept King James II from the throne, and William and Mary were crowned in his place. William and Mary ended religious persecution against nonconformists. Philip Henry resumed preaching publicly. Many of the men who had persecuted nonconformists found themselves out of favor and out of work.

Henry often took pains to help the very people who had caused him so much trouble. "He had learned well," his son wrote, "that great lesson of forgiving and loving enemies."

The new government took steps to right some of the wrongs of the persecution. Officials contacted Philip Henry to find out what had been taken from him and who took it. Henry acknowledged that he lost goods, but he declined to tell them who had taken his property. "I have long since forgiven all from my heart," he wrote the officials, "and have decided never to say anything more about it."

Henry kept preaching and teaching even as his health was failing. His friends pled with him not to push himself too hard. "There is time enough to rest when I am in the grave," he told them. "What were candles made for but to burn?"

His modesty kept him from publishing any of his writings during his lifetime. However, he bequeathed to his children his diaries, letters, and sermons. His son Matthew wrote a famous biography of his father that included many of his diary entries and letters. A collection of his sermons on Colossians 3 became a popular book called *Christ All in All*.

Decades after his death, his daughter said his words continued to nourish her soul. "And what is it he says?" she wrote, "That which his heart was always full of—Christ. Christ! Christ! I think I hear him still: O, make Christ your all."

22

ALEXANDER "SANDY" PEDEN

Covenanter Prophet

(1626–1686)

Late one Sunday night, in 1663, a small congregation in southwestern Scotland wept as they stood around their minister, Sandy Peden. He had just finished a sermon that ran for hours. He urged them to go home, but they clung to him.

For three years, Alexander Peden, or "Sandy" as he was called, had pastored his flock at New Luce, a village nestled in the green hills of Galloway. But this was to be Peden's last service in the church. The king had ordered the ejection of all ministers who refused to acknowledge him as head of the church. Peden and other "outed" ministers were forbidden to come within fifty miles of their congregations and banned from preaching or ministering the sacraments anywhere in the kingdom.

Peden consoled his broken-hearted people saying, "Be calm and trust in God."

Before he left the church, he walked to the pulpit, tapped it with his Bible, and said, "In my Master's name, I charge thee that none ever enter thee but such as enter as I have done by the door."

He meant that no one but a true minister of the Word of God should preach in the church. It happened as Peden charged, for the pulpit remained empty for twenty-five years until the persecution of the crown had ended and a faithful preacher took up the work there again.

Peden bid farewell to his congregation, and slipped away into the night. But he had no intention of abandoning his calling as a minister—he would obey God rather than men.

Sandy Peden wandered the hills and valleys of Scotland proclaiming the good news of Jesus Christ. For twenty-three years he ministered on the run, preaching in fields and sleeping in caves. He baptized by the side of creeks and celebrated the Lord's Supper on rocky crags. He never married, never had a home. Like his Savior, he had no where to lay his head, but he didn't complain. "It is honorable to be a footman in Christ's company, and run at Christ's foot from morning to evening," he said.

People hiked for miles, often in the rain, to a remote glen to hear Peden preach. He spoke a bit haltingly but powerfully. "I observed that every time he spoke," one man said, "whether conversing, reading, praying, or preaching, between every sentence he paused a little, as if he had been hearkening to what the Lord would say to him, or listening to some secret whisper."

Not long after the authorities threw Peden out of his church, they charged him with preaching and baptizing illegally. The crown declared Peden a rebel. If caught, he could be put to death.

Sandy Peden joined other Covenanters whose rallying cry was: "Christ alone is head and king of His Church." The Covenanters disagreed how to respond to the persecution. Some thought they should raise an army and fight the king's troops. Others believed that armed resistance was wrong. In 1666, when Covenanters rose up and marched toward Edinburgh, Peden went with them, preaching to them across the countryside. But as they traveled, Peden came to see that the small, poorly-organized band was headed for slaughter against the king's well-armed troops. He urged them not to go to battle. When the Covenanter militia pressed on, Peden left them. A few days later, they were crushed at the Battle of Rullion Green. Later, one of his friends said to him, "You did well when you left them, seeing that you were persuaded that they would fall and flee before the enemy."

"I should have stayed with them," Peden sighed, "though I would have been cut in pieces."

ALEXANDER "SANDY" PEDEN

"As he fled on horseback with the king's horsemen hard on his heels,
he came to a river, raging with a flood of melted snow."

Whenever Peden preached, he challenged his hearers to cling to Christ and to pray. "It is praying folk alone who will get through the storm," he said.

Peden assured the people that the Lord was always near when they prayed. "If there be one of you, Christ will be the second," he said. "If there be two, He will be the third. You shall never lack company in prayer."

"Where is the Church of Scotland at this day?" he asked in a sermon on the moors. "It is not among the great clergy. I will tell you where the Church is. It is wherever a praying young man or young woman is beside a dike in Scotland. That's where the Church is."

Once he refused to preach for he knew that Covenanters were dying on a battlefield at that very hour. "Let the people go to their prayers," he said, "As for me—I neither can nor will preach any this day; for our friends are fallen and their blood is running like water."

Yet through all the hardship Peden kept an unswerving confidence in God's watch over the Church. Once, when chided that the king would crush the Scottish believers, Peden replied, "I defy the world to steal a lamb of Christ's flock unmissed."

While on the run, he often encouraged himself and others by singing Psalm 32: "Thou art my hiding place; thou shalt keep me from trouble."

Even in the face of all the difficulties, he remained joyful and thankful, quick to smile and the first to build up the discouraged. "His cheerfulness made others cheerful," one man said.

The king's men tried desperately to capture Peden and end his ministry to the people, but countless times the Lord snatched him from their clutches. His breathtaking escapes, told from fireside to fireside across Scotland, warmed the hearts of the beleaguered Covenanters. One spring, dragoons surprised him. As he fled on horseback with the king's horsemen hard on his heels, he came to a river, raging with a flood of melted snow. He plunged in with his horse. As the current rapidly pulled them down river, Peden struggled to cling to his mount. The soldiers halted at the river's edge and dared not follow. They watched from the bank, certain that Peden would be swept to a watery grave. But with strength and skill, he prodded his horse through the icy torrent and up the opposite bank. Soaking wet, he turned in the saddle, smiled and waved to the soldiers. "Lads," he shouted, "you lack my boat for crossing the waters and you will certainly drown. Consider where your landing would be. You are fighting for the devil. O think of it!"

Once, a party of soldiers in search of Peden approached him and a friend on a country road. Peden's friend nearly fainted and feared that they would be captured. But Sandy calmed him. "Keep up your courage and confidence," Peden said, "for God will keep these men from doing us any harm."

As the soldiers came upon them, Peden asked if he could be of assistance. "We are trying to find a spot to cross the river," the captain said.

"Follow me," Peden replied, leading the soldiers down a hillside to a shallow place to ford the river. He watched the troops cross over and received a thankful wave from the captain. "Why did you go with them?" his astonished friend asked.

"It was safe for me," Peden answered, "for my hour of falling into their hands is not yet come."

At another time, a troop of horsemen surprised Sandy Peden and a small group of Covenanters. They fled on foot, darting through heather and briars. They ran quite a distance, but they couldn't shake their pursuers, and they were exhausted. After gaining a little ground by scrambling up a hillside, Peden stopped, gathered the others and said, "Let us pray here; for if the Lord does not hear our prayers and save us, we are all dead men."

He bowed his head and prayed, "Lord, it is thy enemies' day and hour. Lord, cast the lap of thy cloak over old Sandy and these poor ones and save us. And we will remember and praise thy goodness, pity and compassion."

No sooner had Peden finished his prayer than a thick fog blanketed the hillside. The soldiers could barely see their hands in front of their faces. They gave up the chase. The Covenanters slipped away to preach and pray another day.

He did not always escape. While spending the night in the home of a friend, Peden was captured and hauled to Edinburgh to stand trial. The court condemned him to the prison on Bass Rock, a stony island in the Firth of Forth, a hellish place where many prisoners died from the harsh conditions.

"We are not permitted to talk, to gather or to worship together," Peden wrote a friend. "We are locked up day and night to hear only the sighs and groans of our fellow prisoners. O for grace to thank Him in whatever service He places us, whether in bonds or freedom."

He loved to watch the birds soaring over the island prison. "They call on us to bless God for his mercies," he said. But he also confessed he envied the freedom that the birds enjoyed.

One day as Peden walked in the prison yard, a guard shouted at him, "The devil take you."

"Poor man," Peden said to him, "you don't know what you are saying; but you shall repent of it."

Peden's reply cut the man to the quick and he seemed to lose his senses. As another guard led him away, he called for Peden's help. "The devil will come immediately and take me away," he cried.

Later, Sandy Peden sought out the guard. He found the man wrestling under a deep sense of his sin. Peden led him to trust in Christ for forgiveness. The next day, the guard did not report for duty. When his commander ordered him to take his weapon and watch the prisoners, he refused, "I will lift no arms against Jesus Christ and His people," he said. "I have done that for too long."

The warden threatened him with death if he did not do his guard duty. "Though you tear me in pieces," he said, "I shall never lift arms in that way again."

Stripped of his rank and expelled from the service, the man returned home and lived the rest of his life as a faithful Christian.

For four years, Peden endured the brutal life on Bass Rock. Then he was moved to the Tolbooth, a ghastly prison in Edinburgh. "A grave for men alive," some called it. After fifteen months, he and sixty other Covenanters were banished to America, doomed to work as slaves on the plantations of Virginia, never to return to Scotland under pain of death. Guards marched the prisoners to the coast and put them on a ship. Many of them wept, believing they would never see their homeland again. "Be of good cheer," Peden told them. "The ship has not been built that will carry us over the sea to any of the plantations."

They sailed to London where they were to be transferred to a convict ship bound for America. "You need not fear," Peden told his companions. "Lift up your hearts for the day of your redemption draws near. In London we will all be set free."

What Peden predicted came to pass. The captain of the convict ship at dock in London, expecting a gang of Scottish thieves, refused to take on board the good Christian men who were being punished for their faith. He set them free. Peden and the others walked back to Scotland.

The years of exposure to the weather and the harsh conditions of prison took a toll on Sandy Peden. His gray, wrinkled, and stooped body made him look far older than he was. When Peden lay dying in a cave near his boyhood home, he sent for James Renwick, a bold, twenty-three-year-old preacher. Peden and Renwick had never met, yet Peden had formed a bad opinion of Renwick based on what others had told him. Renwick came at once and found Peden, pale and weak. Peden propped himself up on his elbow and looked at him. "Sir," he asked, "are you the Mr. James Renwick that there is so much noise about?"

"Father," he answered, "my name is James Renwick; but I have given the world no grounds to make noise about me, for I have taught no new principles or practices, but what our Reformers and Covenanters have held."

"Sit down, sir," Peden said, "and tell me about your conversion and your call to the ministry."

Renwick told him how God had saved his soul and led him into preaching. He gave God the glory for the fruit of his work in the lives of others. When he finished, Peden said, "You have answered me to my soul's satisfaction, and I am very sorry that I should have believed any ill reports of you. But, sir, before you go, you must pray for me; for I am old and going to leave the world."

Renwick kneeled and poured out his heart to God for Peden. Then Peden took his hand and embraced him. "Sir," he said, "I find you a faithful servant to your Master. Go on depending on the Lord alone."

Shortly before he died, Peden said, "God has been good and kind to poor old Sandy through a long tract of time." He looked forward to the sleep of Christ. "That I might have quiet in my grave," he said, "for I have had little in my life."

Sandy Peden died in the winter of 1686, worn out at the age of sixty. His friends secretly buried him in the churchyard not far from his childhood home. But soldiers discovered the spot and dug up his body. Seeking to dishonor and punish him even in death, they carried it to a hillside in the village of Cumnock where prisoners were executed. They buried him, like a common criminal, at the foot of the gallows. In the years that followed, the people of Cumnock stopped using the church graveyard and began to bury their dead on the hillside that they might lay beside Sandy Peden. As one Scot later wrote, "That spot has become the hallowed God's Acre, where in the midst of his own kith and kin, the prophet of the Lord sleeps until the Resurrection Day."

23

RICHARD CAMERON

Lion of the Covenant

(1644–1680)

On a late afternoon in 1680 in the Central Lowlands of Scotland, two armed groups faced one another across a marshy field. On one side, far larger and better equipped, were the dragoons, soldiers of King Charles II, who had been tracking their enemy for months. On the other side of the field stood a small band of men, fewer than sixty in number. Poorly armed, they were not professional soldiers, but farmers and tradesmen most with no horses to ride into battle. Their leader was not a military commander but a minister. They were Covenanters led by Richard Cameron, the Lion of the Covenant.[1]

The Covenanters resisted the king when he pressured the Christians of Scotland to worship in ways not of their own choosing. "Christ alone is the Head of the Church," the Covenanters proclaimed.

Richard Cameron had never dreamed that he would lead troops into battle against the king. He had lived the quiet life of a school teacher until he went out to the countryside to hear a field preacher at a conventicle, an illegal worship service conducted by a minister

---

1. "Richard Cameron: Lion of the Covenant" is excerpted from Richard M. Hannula's *Trial and Triumph: Stories from Church History* (Moscow, ID: Canon Press, 1999).

thrown out of his church for disobeying the king's orders. Richard Cameron heard about Jesus and became a believer.

Not long after, Cameron became a lay preacher, leading others to turn to Christ for the forgiveness of their sins. But the king's men were jailing, torturing, and sometimes killing preachers, so Cameron and hundreds of others fled across the sea to Holland. There he studied the Bible intensely and was ordained a minister. Cameron was determined to return even if it meant certain death. Before he left Holland, a Scottish minister placed his hand on Cameron's head and cried out, "Behold, here is the head of a faithful minister and servant of Jesus Christ, who shall lose his head for his Master's interest, and it shall be set up before sun and moon, in the view of the world."

After returning secretly to Scotland, he preached in the hills, marshes, and fields. And he witnessed the cruelties that the Covenanters and their families suffered at the hands of the king's troops. They whipped women, flogged boys, stole livestock, and plundered houses and fields—reducing many of the poor Scots to starvation. Some Covenanters were shot on sight. Many more were arrested, tortured, and executed. Others were shipped off to the Caribbean plantations as slaves.

Seeing the barbarity of the king's soldiers, Richard Cameron and his brother, Michael, and some other brave men joined together to fight the oppressors of Scotland. Though poorly armed and trained, they vowed to defend the innocent men, women, and children of Scotland. "Be not discouraged at the fewness of your number," Cameron told his followers, "for when Christ comes to raise up His own work in Scotland, He will not lack men enough to work for Him."

Refusing to hide their intentions, they rode boldly into the town square of Sanquhar on June 22, 1680, sang a psalm, said a prayer, and read a declaration: "We disown Charles Stuart, who has been reigning, or rather tyrannizing, on the throne of Britain for many years. He has no right to the crown of Scotland for he has lied and broken his covenant both to God and His Church. We being under the standard of our Lord Jesus Christ, Captain of Salvation, do declare a war with the tyrant and all his men, as enemies of our Lord Jesus Christ."

King Charles ordered a large reward for the capture of Richard Cameron, dead or alive. Although hunted throughout the land, no one told the soldiers Cameron's whereabouts. Even on the run, he continued to preach and lead services.

Finally, the king's soldiers caught up with Richard Cameron and his band. Before the battle began, Cameron bowed his head, raised his voice, and led his men in prayer one last time asking the Lord to protect the lives of those who were not yet ready to die. "Spare the green and take the ripe," he prayed.

He turned to his faithful brother, "Come Michael," he said, "let us fight it out to the last; for this is the day that I have longed for, to die fighting against our Lord's enemies; and this is the day that we shall get the crown."

Richard strengthened his friends saying, "Be encouraged all of you to fight it out valiantly, for all of you who fall this day I see heaven's gates cast wide open to receive them."

Together, they sang a final song of praise to God and then the dragoons attacked—their horses' hoof beats thundering across the field, their halberds and swords flashing. Though greatly outnumbered, the Covenanters fought bravely. But when the battle was ended, Richard and Michael Cameron and several of their men lay dead.

The soldiers cut off Richard's head and hands and brought them as trophies to the king's council at Edinburgh. As they entered the city, a soldier hoisted Cameron's head high on the tip of his lance shouting, "Here is the head of a traitor and a rebel."

The council ordered that Cameron's head and hands be set high in a prominent place in Edinburgh as a warning to anyone who dared resist the king. Before the head and hands were set in place, the king's men performed a final act of cruelty. Cameron's father was in prison for supporting the cause of the Covenanters. Soldiers went to his cell and dropped the hands and head into his lap. "Do you know them?" they asked.

"I know them, I know them," he said kissing the head and hands. "They are my son's, my own dear son's."

Overcome with grief he broke down and wept. "It is the Lord," he said through his tears. "Good is the will of the Lord, who cannot wrong me nor mine, but has made goodness and mercy to follow us all our days."

Even Richard Cameron's enemies admired his faith and courage and that of his father and brother. One who saw his head mounted in

Edinburgh said, "There are the head and hands of a man who lived praying and preaching and died praying and fighting."

Eight more years of bitter persecution awaited the Covenanters before the Glorious Revolution swept away the Stuart kings from the throne forever. Even though thousands more were killed for the faith, the life and death of Richard Cameron shone as one of the brightest lights for Christ during those dark days of persecution.

24

JOHN FLAVEL

For the Glory of God and the Souls of Men

(1627–1691)

It was 1665 and the townspeople of Dartmouth, England, slowly walked the road out of town with their minister. Old folks and children—men and women—wept as they went. One by one they came along side the Reverend John Flavel and took him by the hand to say goodbye. Tears streamed down Pastor Flavel's cheeks too. When they reached the churchyard at the edge of town, Flavel tried to encourage them, but he could hardly be heard over the mournful cries of his congregation.

Three years earlier, King Charles II made all ministers in the kingdom pledge their full agreement with the Church of England's government and teachings. When John Flavel and two thousand other Puritan pastors refused to conform to the unbiblical demands, they were expelled from their churches.

The king and his bishops thought that this would stop the influence of the Puritan ministers, but they were wrong. Although the bishop put a new minister in the Dartmouth church, the people still looked to Flavel as their pastor. Since he was barred from the church's pulpit, they crowded into his home to hear him preach. At all hours of the day and night they came to him for spiritual counsel. The same thing happened with other expelled ministers throughout

England. Angry that they kept teaching the people, the king's government made it illegal for expelled ministers to come within five miles of their churches. And so John Flavel had to leave Dartmouth or face arrest.

As he walked out of the city, he thought about the ten years that he had preached to his people and visited them in their homes. "I will teach nothing to you, but Jesus Christ," he had told them. "Christ shall be the center of all my ministry."

Flavel loved to teach them about the Savior. "Of all the subjects in the world," he said, "the preaching of Jesus Christ is the sweetest." He worked hard to prepare sermons that would show his flock the glories of Jesus Christ and the holy life Christ called them to live. He believed that unless a minister felt each sermon in his own heart, it would not help his hearers. John Flavel felt his sermons.

His reputation as a faithful preacher spread quickly. Believers throughout southwestern England came to Dartmouth to hear him proclaim the good news of Jesus Christ. "I cannot say enough about his excellent preaching," a member of his congregation said. "A person must have a very soft head or a very hard heart who could sit under his ministry and not be changed."

After he was banished from the city, he lived in a village several miles from Dartmouth, but he kept caring for his flock. Often, he stole into Dartmouth to visit his people from house to house. He preached twice every Lord's Day—sometimes in homes and sometimes in fields. This was very dangerous because preaching without the king's permission was against the law. Agents of the king declared him an outlaw and pursued him like hounds on a fox.

Once, a large group gathered in some woods to hear Flavel preach. But word of the meeting leaked out, and the king's soldiers burst upon them when he was in the middle of his sermon. As the soldiers tried to push through the crowd to capture him, the people blocked them. He escaped along with most of the congregation, but some were arrested. Those who escaped did not scatter and run home. To Flavel's surprise, they led him to another wood where he finished his sermon to the great blessing of his hearers.

For years he ministered on the run, preaching in homes and barns, on the beach and in the woods. Losing his house and salary did not throw him into despair. "Christ is the very center of all delights and pleasures," he said. Flavel believed that all the hardships that expelled ministers suffered made them more faithful. "We were reduced by a blessed necessity to live the life of faith," he said, "so now we are better prepared for the work than ever before."

The king's men tried desperately to capture him, but the Lord kept him out of their clutches. One time soldiers surprised him as he preached at the seashore. They nearly laid hands on him when he leapt on a horse and rode away. Hot on his heels, they chased him until Flavel galloped his horse across a miry mudflat and into the ocean. The soldiers dared not follow.

Once, policemen raided a prayer meeting that Flavel was leading. When they barged through the front door to arrest him, he escaped out the back. His father (a nonconformist preacher) and his mother were not so fortunate. Not long after Flavel was banished from Dartmouth, his father and mother were captured. Shortly after being thrown into a prison infected with the plague, they died.

In 1672, the king permitted nonconformist ministers to return to their cities and preach. John Flavel went back at once to Dartmouth. Wanting to make the most of the opportunity, he worked night and day preaching and counseling and visiting his people. "He spent himself in the work of God," one friend said of him.

During this time, a ship docked at Dartmouth's port. On board was a twenty-three-year-old seafarer who had long suffered from deep depression. In his despair, he wounded himself so badly that doctors were called to save him. They stitched him up, but they did not think that he would live through the day. Someone called John Flavel to visit him. He asked the young man about his faith. "I hope that God will grant me eternal life," the young man said in a weak voice.

"I fear your hopes are not well grounded," Flavel told him. Then he explained that every man is a sinner and that God hates and punishes sin. As the seafarer began to understand that he was a rebel against God, he broke down in tears. "I see the evil of my sins like I never saw them before!" he said. Then looking up at Flavel, he asked, "Is there any hope for me now?"

"There might be," he answered. Then he told the dying man the good news of forgiveness in Jesus Christ. He explained that Jesus took the punishment for sins upon himself on the cross. "Christ seeks to win sinners to himself," Flavel said. "Put your trust in Him."

"Though I am very late," the young man whispered, "pray for me that I might sincerely repent of my sins and believe in Christ."

As Flavel began to pray out loud, it pleased God to fill the seafarer's heart with a living faith in Jesus. Although he was exhausted and wracked with pain, he asked Jesus Christ to rescue him from his sins. Flavel assured him that Christ never turns away anyone who comes to Him in faith. He sat for some time by the young man's bedside and encouraged him. After a while, John Flavel rose to leave, but the man gripped his arm and begged him to stay.

Flavel told him that he had to go, but he promised to return later. "Cling to Christ and pray," he told him. As he left the ship, he thought he would never see the man alive in this world again. But when he came back that evening, the young man was waiting for him. He did not have the strength to do anything but lie on his back. But nothing pleased him more than to hear Flavel talk about Jesus. "Christ is a sea of sweetness without one drop of bitterness," Flavel told him.

"Sir," the seafarer said with tears welling in his eyes, "I believe that the Lord has forgiven all my other sins, but one thing still troubles me. I doubt that the sin I committed this day will be pardoned. Will Jesus Christ forgive me who has shed my own blood?"

"The Lord Jesus Christ shed His blood for even greater sins than yours," Flavel answered. "The vilest sinner will find free grace in Christ."

The man's pale face brightened and he said, "I cast myself upon Christ. Let Him do what He will with me."

Remarkably, over time the young man's wounds fully healed. Flavel spent many hours with him during the weeks of his recovery. After the man returned to his home town, Flavel received a letter from his minister. He thanked Flavel for leading the seafarer to Christ and told him that his faith was growing. "If ever a great and thorough work of God was done in a heart," the minister wrote, "it was done in that man."

After a year of freedom to minister, the king again banned nonconformists from preaching. John Flavel was forced to leave Dartmouth, but he kept preaching in secret.

As the persecution against the nonconformists grew hotter, it became too dangerous for him to remain near Dartmouth. Flavel decided it would be better to go to London where he was not well known. He hoped to blend into the huge city and have more freedom to preach and teach. He boarded a ship bound for London—a few days sail away.

Not long after the ship set out to sea, a fierce storm arose. Huge waves violently tossed the ship and pounded over the deck. Riggings broke and sails ripped. The captain and crew feared for their lives. "Unless God changes the weather," one sailor said, "there is no hope."

Flavel called some of the crewmen into the cabin to pray. The heaving ship threw them from one side of the cabin to the other. Waves crashed over the bow and rushed into the cabin. Flavel braced himself against a wooden pillar. With seawater nearly covering his boots, he called out to God. "Lord, have mercy on me and all who are in this ship," he prayed. "Heavenly Father, if I and this company should perish in this storm, the name of God will be blasphemed. The enemies of our holy faith will say, 'Although he escaped arrest onshore, yet God has overtaken him at sea.'"

He finished his prayer full of hope that God would rescue them. Just moments after he stopped praying, a sailor burst into the cabin shouting, "Deliverance! Deliverance! God hears prayer! The wind has turned fair."

Everyone in the cabin scrambled up the stairs to the deck. To their amazement, they found the winds and waves had died down. They thanked God for His mercy. The grateful crew safely guided the ship to London.

For a few years, John Flavel preached to small groups in London and he wrote books. He wrote to deepen the love of Christians for their Savior, and called them to respond to God's grace by living joyful and obedient lives in Christ. Many people found great wisdom and encouragement in his writings.

It happened one day in London that a wealthy gentleman entered the bookshop owned by a Mr. Boulter. The gentleman wanted to read something for fun. He asked if the shop had books of plays. "We do not," Mr. Boulter replied. "But I think you would like this book by John Flavel called *Keeping the Heart*. I assure you that it will do you more good than reading a play."

The man took the book and glanced at the first few pages. Then his face grew red and he shouted, "What kind of fanatic wrote this book?"

"Sir," Boulter said, "there is no cause to criticize the book or the author. Read it and you will see."

"I will buy it," the gentleman said, "but I won't read it."

"What will you do with it then?" asked Mr. Boulter.

"I will tear it up and burn it and send it to the devil," the man growled.

"If that is the case," Mr. Boulter replied, "I will not sell it to you."

"Alright, I will read it, but I won't like it," he said.

"If you read it and don't like it," Mr. Boulter told him, "bring it back and I will refund your money."

Several weeks later, the gentleman came back to the shop carrying the book. "Sir," the man said to Mr. Boulter with a beaming smile, "I most heartily thank you for putting this book into my hands. I bless God that He moved you to do it. It has saved my soul. Blessed be God that I came into your shop!"

Then the gentleman bought one hundred copies of the book. "I am going to give them to the poor who cannot afford to buy it for themselves," he said.

The man left the bookshop, praising God.

John Flavel's life and his writings inspired generations of Christians in Britain and America, including the Great Awakening preachers Jonathan Edwards and George Whitefield. One of Flavel's friends summed up his life well: "He was always thinking about the glory of God and the souls of men."

25

JAMES FRASER OF BREA

Full of the Consolations of Christ

(1639–1699)

In 1665, a tidal wave of debt swept over James Fraser. He had inherited the debts from his deceased father, a fearless Covenanter leader but a careless financial steward. The estate of Brea on the Black Isle in the far north of Scotland had been in the Fraser family for generations. Now creditors controlled nearly all the family's lands and property. Once revered, the Frasers were now held in contempt. Even extended family members and friends kept their distance. Tongues wagged saying the Frasers were getting their just deserts for being "religious fanatics." The mocking comments, James said, "wound my heart as a sword."

Financial woes consumed his thoughts and filled his heart with bitterness. Fraser, an earnest Christian, knew his attitude was displeasing to God. Again and again he confessed his sin and sought to repent. "As time went on," Fraser said, "and as I more and more learned to take all these things immediately from God's hand to me, I came to see that all my circumstances were the very best possible for me and for God's purposes with me."

Whenever complaints about his dire situation entered his mind, he stopped his thoughts and prayed, "No, Lord! Not my rebellious will, but Thy holy will alone!"

James Fraser saw God using his trials to sanctify him. "The Lord is humbling my heart," he wrote, "breaking my pride, working to deaden me to the world and increasing my faith and patience. I drew nearer to God and was able to say, 'It is good for me that I have been afflicted.'"

Even the rejection of his friends lost some of its sting. "While others would revile me and look down upon me and taunt me," Fraser said, "the Lord would draw near."

Over many years of stress and hard work, Fraser managed to pay off most of the debts and regain some of the family's lands.

Since his college days at the University of Edinburgh, Fraser felt God's call to the ministry, but at that time Presbyterianism had been made illegal in Scotland and only bishops had the power to license anyone to preach. The bishops, under the direction of King Charles II, sought to destroy the Presbyterians who held to the doctrines and practices of the Scottish Reformation. "Godly ministers were deposed," Fraser reported, "and wicked scandalous ministers set up in their places. Godliness was a crime. Lord, what a world was this!"

James Fraser refused to acknowledge the bishops as the rightful heads of the Church of Scotland, so his way to the ministry was blocked. He returned home to manage the family estate. But the call to preach never left him. The Word of God was, Fraser said, "as a fire within me." He started to preach to his own household at Brea, and then friends asked him to preach in their homes. Before long, large crowds jammed into country manors to hear him. Eventually, he was ordained as a gospel preacher by the Field Presbytery of Moray, a group of Presbyterian ministers and elders in northern Scotland who carried on the Reformed faith in secret. They were called the Field Presbytery because they had no church buildings to use, so they worshipped in houses and fields. The government called these clandestine worship services "conventicles" and made it a crime punishable by death to preach at them. When Fraser began preaching fulltime he said, "Ecstasy of joy filled my heart."

Fraser's Christ-centered preaching won him a great following. Hundreds came to hear him in the cities and thousands in the countryside. He stuck to the heart of the gospel in all his messages. "To draw souls to and build them up in Christ Jesus," he said, "is the great end and scope of all faithful ministers. Christ is the alpha and omega of preaching."

Seeking to stop Fraser in his tracks, the authorities summoned him to court for preaching at conventicles. Knowing that the court would most certainly cast him into jail, he chose not to appear. The king's government denounced him as an outlaw.

This began a life of living on the run—preaching in homes, barns, and fields. Several times soldiers nearly had him in their grasp, but he managed to escape in the nick of time.

Still more trials were in store for him. In October 1676, after four years of marriage, his wife died. "The Lord who gave took away from me the delight of my eyes with all earthly joys," Fraser said. "The whole world looked to me as an empty ghastly room, despoiled of its best furnishing."

Although he lived another twenty years, he never married again.

At that time the Covenanters were divided. Some favored armed resistance against their persecutors. Others, like Fraser, believed that it was wrong to resist with violence. "Some hotheads were for taking the sword against their oppressors," Fraser said, "but I opposed rising in arms all I could and preached against it."

Fraser's popularity angered the government officials who placed a large ransom on his head. A few months after his wife's death, an official in Edinburgh learned from a servant girl that James Fraser often stayed in the house of her master in the city. He bribed the woman to inform him when Fraser arrived again at the house. In January 1677, Fraser was captured in his friend's home and carried off to prison.

The next evening, guards brought Fraser before the Scottish Privy Council. Archbishop Sharp acted as Fraser's primary accuser, charging James Fraser with field preaching and supporting armed rebellion against the king.

"Have you preached at conventicles?" Sharp asked Fraser.

"I do preach frequently, as the Lord called me, and independently of the bishop," Fraser answered. "But the subjects of my sermons were not disloyal or traitorous as you allege. I preached repentance towards God and faith towards Jesus Christ. I never stirred up the people to sedition."

"These conventicles are rendezvous of rebellion and are contrary to the king's law," Sharp said.

"I do not think it unlawful to preach the gospel either in houses or fields," Fraser replied.

"This gentleman holds the most pernicious principles," Sharp said, "and is very active in spreading them. I scarcely hear of a conventicle where Mr. Fraser is not the preacher."

"I hold no pernicious principles," Fraser responded. "I have been preaching Christ and exhorting people to mend their ways and repent, and if doing that is pernicious I confess myself guilty of it."

Although some in the council were willing to let Fraser go, the archbishop insisted that he be punished as an enemy of the king. Early the next morning, the jailor awoke Fraser and shouted, "Get up and get ready! You are going to the Bass."

A guard of soldiers led Fraser down to the harbor and placed him on board a ship that took him two miles from shore to the prison on Bass Rock. King Charles II used the island prison to house some of the leading Covenanters and others that he considered enemies of the state. The prisoners survived on scant rations of dried fish. Rain water or melted snow collected in puddles was their only source of drinking water. In stormy weather, boats could not bring supplies and the prisoners nearly starved. The vile and dank air of the cells gave rise to lung infections and a host of other ailments. "To this melancholy place I came," Fraser wrote later, "and continued there in prison for two and a half years."

To be wrenched from friends, family, and his ministry was a bitter trial, but God was with him. "In my darkness the Lord of light was round about me," he reported. "They could not shut Him out from me."

Fraser had often exhorted others saying, "Never be idle. Never sit still. Be always in duty, never quit."

On the Bass, he took his own advice. Fraser set aside time each day to confess his sins and repent. He meditated on the Bible, especially the passages about Christ's suffering for sinners. He studied Hebrew and Greek and gained some skill in them. Fraser held days of fasting and prayer which he called "my sweetest seasons and best times." Twice a day he gathered with some fellow prisoners to worship God, to hear a sermon and sing psalms of praise. He read books on theology and he wrote a treatise on God's plan to save sinners. "I had some special visits from God and some further discoveries of the knowledge of Christ and the gospel that I never had before," Fraser said.

He continued his practice of keeping a spiritual journal where he carefully recorded the ups and downs of his life of faith—his pursuit of holiness and God's grace to him. "I am taken up with observing providences," he wrote, "especially in reference to myself, to see what God may be doing in them, but, above all, to see God's wisdom, holiness and love in them."

The Covenanters and Puritans were great students of God's work in the souls of believers, and James Fraser was one of the most insightful of them all. In his journal he recounted nineteen marks of growth in grace, twenty-seven evidences of regeneration, twenty-five things that had done him good, thirteen devices of Satan exposed, and on and on. However, his meditations always brought him back to his Savior. "I learned to live less and less in myself and on myself and more and more on Jesus Christ," Fraser wrote.

Once, the Scottish Privy Council offered to free Fraser if he would promise to obey the law and not preach. Fraser declined the offer. Eventually the king ordered the release of all prisoners that had not been actively involved in rebellion against the Crown. In August 1679, Fraser and a number of other Covenanter ministers were taken out of the Bass to Edinburgh and given their freedom. Field preaching remained illegal, but preaching in private homes was not against the law.

Fraser immediately resumed preaching. For two years he went from house to house, living with different families and preaching forgiveness in Jesus Christ. In November 1681, Fraser preached to a large crowd in a barn. The Privy Council in Edinburgh got word of it and summoned him to stand trial. The council charged him with preaching in the fields and inciting rebellion against the king. Fraser told them that he only preached the good news of Jesus Christ. He admitted that he preached in homes and barns. "But," Fraser added, "I have not preached in any field since leaving the Bass. I never opposed the bishops or the king with anything but spiritual weapons."

The council declared him guilty of rebellion, levied a large fine against him, and sent him to Blackness Prison. Six months later, the council banished him from Scotland. The sentence broke his heart. "Shall I leave and never see mother, children, brethren, sisters, and kindly friends," Fraser said, "and spend the rest of my days among strangers?"

As he sailed for London in May 1682, Fraser poured out his fears to the Lord and this Scripture promise sprang into his mind: "Surely goodness and mercy shall follow me all the days of my life."

In London, Fraser doubted that he would have the opportunity to preach, but soon he was invited to speak in many different places. For a full year, he preached nearly every morning and evening in homes and every Lord's Day in Independent churches. "I prayed, read, and expounded Scripture twice a day," Fraser wrote, "and thus continued until July 21, 1683, when I was apprehended."

The authorities in London arrested Fraser under the suspicion that he was involved in a plot to assassinate the king. He stood before the English Privy Council with the king in attendance. It was the first time Fraser came face to face with the man who had persecuted the Covenanters so violently. When asked what he knew about the conspiracy to kill the king, Fraser answered, "I knew nothing of a plot against his Majesty. I stand against all violent attempts against his Majesty or his government."

Fraser courteously but boldly defended the faith of the Reformation before the king. But when he refused to take the Oxford Oath which bound every man not to endeavor to reform the government of the church, the council condemned him to prison. His incarceration at Newgate Prison was a double burden because the jailor forbade him visitors and would not permit him to preach to his fellow prisoners. Despite the hardships, Fraser declared, "Here I experienced the Lord's goodness and mercy which never left me."

After the Glorious Revolution in 1688 swept away the oppressive Stuart kings, the persecution of Covenanters ended. Fraser returned to Scotland and became the minister of Culross in Fife where he served for ten years until he died at the age of fifty-nine. His last words were: "I am full of the consolations of Christ."

After his death, his journals were published. For the last 300 years, the *Memoirs of James Fraser of Brea* has brought great blessing to countless readers. Believers undergoing trials or wrestling with doubts and fears have found Fraser's insights into Christ, grace, and holiness a healing balm for their souls.

26

ROBERT TRAILL AND ROBERT TRAILL JR.

Covenanter Father and Son

(1602–c. 1670 and 1642–1716)

The 1660s were dark days for the Scottish Covenanters. They had hoped for better things when Charles II was crowned king in London in 1660. At that time, the Reverend Robert Traill, pastor of the famous Greyfriars Kirk in Edinburgh, his friend James Guthrie and eight other Scottish ministers wrote the new king a letter. They congratulated him on his coronation and reminded Charles of his solemn pledge to protect the religious freedom of the Church of Scotland. But Charles had no intention of honoring his promise, and he resented anyone who held him to account. So agents of the king arrested Traill and his nine friends and cast them in the dungeon of Edinburgh Castle. After seven months they were released, but were watched closely by the king's spies.

In the meantime, King Charles II and his Scottish Parliament sought control of the Church of Scotland. They rescinded the Covenants—documents that affirmed the church's right to be free from interference by the Crown. The king declared himself the supreme judge of church affairs and forced the rule of bishops—chosen by the king—on the Scottish church. Any minister who refused to swear allegiance to these changes was cast out of his church and house and forbidden to preach anywhere in the kingdom. Hundreds of pastors chose to lose all their earthly possessions rather than submit to the king's control of the Kirk. Among them was Robert Traill.

Traill, and many others like him, preached secretly in cottages and in the countryside. Then one Sunday afternoon, agents of the king heard that Traill was preaching in the home of a friend where Traill and his family were staying. Constables arrested him.

When in 1662, the Reverend Traill stood trial before a committee of the Scottish Parliament; he defended himself against accusations of disloyalty to the king. And he pled for the persecuted church in the land. "I must in all humility beg leave to entreat your lordships," he said, "that you seriously consider what you do with poor ministers who have been so long kept from their liberty to preach the gospel. And so many congregations are laid desolate for so long a time and many poor souls have been deprived of a word of comfort from their ministers in the hour of their greatest need."

Traill's words had no affect. They banished him forever from Scotland. When he left for Holland, the tearful parting from his wife Jean and six children broke his heart. His family suffered terribly from the loss of husband and father. But Jean Traill, buoyed by Robert's letters of encouragement, did not abandon the principles of her exiled husband.

"Take courage, my dear heart," Traill wrote her. "The storm has scattered our poor family, but blessed be our Lord that we may often meet before God's throne in prayer. Fret not about unjust men who have driven me so far away from you; but pray for them. I am sure you would rather have me in banishment far from you, than have me at home with you as a bishop or dean or timeserving minister."

Jean, clinging fast to her faith and the Scottish Covenants, hosted secret worship meetings. Robert Traill asked her to nourish the faith of their sons and daughters. "Take care of our children," he wrote, "see what good you can do for their souls in praying for them and admonishing them in the Lord. And when I come to fall asleep and to be taken off the stage, I hope there shall be a family serving the Lord in their generation better than ever I did in mine."

"Make it your daily task to seek the Lord and to serve Him with all your hearts," he wrote in a letter to his children. "Read the Scriptures frequently and pray for faith to believe all the great and precious promises that are breathed out in the Scriptures. There is room enough for all of you in heaven—there is mercy and grace enough in Jesus Christ to bring you there."

To his son Robert who was preparing to be a minister, he wrote, "Let not this storm shake you or make you quit your purpose. It would be a great part of my joy to see you a preacher of the truth." Young Robert embraced his father's faith—even bravely attending James Guthrie when Guthrie was put to death on the gallows in Edinburgh.

In 1665, the authorities imprisoned Jean Traill for a time for the crime of writing and receiving letters from her husband.

Things got worse a few months later. The king's men had banned many Christian books written by Covenanters and Puritans and ordered all copies turned over to the authorities to be burned by hangmen. Knowing the Traills' strong Covenanter loyalties, constables ransacked their home and discovered a banned book. The Traills went into hiding to avoid arrest.

The persecution of the Covenanters grew so fierce that some Scots took up arms to fight back. At the Battle of Rullion Green, the king's well armed and trained troops easily crushed the ill-prepared Scots. Many Covenanters were killed on the field or captured. The government suspected that young Robert Traill had fought for the Covenanters in the battle. They proclaimed him an outlaw and ordered his arrest. In January 1667, Robert fled to Holland where he joined his father and hundreds of other Scots who had been banished or had fled the persecution.

Robert Traill Jr. took up his theological studies in Holland. Robert helped an exiled Scottish minister publish a book by the well-known Covenanter, Samuel Rutherford. Not long after, Robert's father died.

In 1670, Traill moved to England and was ordained as a Presbyterian minister. In all his labors as a minister he sought to point people to Jesus Christ for the forgiveness of their sins. "Embrace the offer of the grace of God," he told his flock. "In the gospel, Christ is freely offered and freely given. Welcome Him and receive Him with thanksgiving and joy."

After preaching in England for several years, he longed to return to his homeland to minister to the beleaguered Scots. So Traill crossed the border into Scotland where he preached to small groups who gathered in secret.

"Come to Christ and believe in Him," Traill said, "Don't delay when you are offered the grace of God. As the Holy Spirit says, 'Today if you will hear his voice, harden not your hearts.' You may not hear his voice tomorrow; hardness of heart grows mightily by delays."

In the summer of 1677, the authorities caught him preaching in a house in Edinburgh and arrested him. They condemned him to Bass Rock—the notorious island prison where many inmates died from the wretched conditions.

On Bass Rock, Traill befriended Alexander Peden and James Fraser of Brea and other imprisoned Covenanters. After three months of incarceration in the Bass dungeon, he was released and banished from Scotland. Traill went to London where he became the pastor of a Presbyterian church.

In the 1690s, a heated debate arose among the churches of England. Some ministers had begun to teach that Christ's cross opened the way for sinners to get to heaven, but after believing in Christ, Christians earned their salvation through good works. Robert Traill declared that believers are saved by the grace of God only through the work of Christ. "Believing in Jesus Christ is no work," Traill said, "but a resting on Jesus Christ. The poor wearied sinner can never believe in Jesus Christ till he finds he can do nothing for himself—every man is hopeless and helpless in himself."

"My friends," Traill preached, "consider this—our Lord Jesus Christ did not die to make hard things easy, to make a hard way to heaven easy. But Christ died to make impossible things certain. He did not die to make it easier to get to heaven than it was before; but he died to make certain a way to heaven that was impossible before."

God's grace in Christ was his constant theme. "You have heard that the grace of God shines gloriously in the justification of a sinner by the righteousness of Christ," Traill said in a sermon. "In all your dealings with God, think much of grace—bring nothing with you in your hand, offer nothing to God for your justification; it is a free gift."

Robert Traill served his congregation in London for nearly forty years until he died in 1716 at the age of seventy-four. After his death, friends collected and published many of his sermons. A century later, a prominent minister, after reading Traill's thoughts on a Bible passage, wrote in his diary: "That text was never more sweet and pleasant to me than today. I bless the Lord who directed that honest man to preach and write. And I bless the Lord who brought his book to my hand and directed me to read it this day. I read with tears of joy."

Traill's sermons, overflowing with biblical wisdom and holy joy, still inspire believers today.

27

JOHN NISBET

Farmer and Fighter

(1627–1685)

As darkness fell on a cold November night in 1666, John Nisbet awoke, felt his wounds, and groaned. He weakly raised his head and saw the bodies of his slain comrades scattered around him. Earlier that day, Nisbet and a ragtag, poorly-armed band of Covenanters had fought the king's well-equipped troops. They had clashed on Rullion Green, a field in the Pentland Hills near Edinburgh, Scotland.

The royal troops slaughtered many Covenanters and took others prisoners. Nisbet suffered multiple wounds and passed out on the battlefield. His enemies, taking him for dead, stripped him of his sword and clothes and left him to rot on the ground. But hours later, he came to and under the cover of darkness, he crawled away and escaped. After many months of recuperation under his wife's watchful care, his wounds healed.

Not all of the most memorable Covenanters were ministers. Some were cobblers, blacksmiths, and merchants—but most were farmers like John Nisbet. Nisbet was born into an earnest Christian family. Before the Reformation came to Scotland in the 1560s, the Nisbets had been Lollards, the persecuted people who worshipped God according to the Scriptures. Their greatest family treasure was a 200-year-old, hand-written copy of the New Testament that his ancestors used to hide in a vault under the house.

During his boyhood, Nisbet studied the Scriptures, memorizing large sections of it. He came to understand and believe all that Jesus Christ had done for him. "Christ forgave me and redeemed me!" he exclaimed, "Christ created me anew."

As a tall, broad-shouldered and athletic young man, Nisbet became a soldier. He crossed the sea and fought in Germany to protect the Protestant Reformation in Europe. When he returned from war, he began working the large farm he inherited called Hardhill. It was located in Loudoun Parish, Ayrshire in western Scotland. He married, and he and his wife Margaret had four children—three boys and one girl. He wanted nothing more than to live a quiet life with his family, but that was not to be.

Not long after King Charles II came to the throne in 1660, he—and a compliant Scottish Parliament—abolished all the laws supporting the independence of the Church of Scotland. Bishops appointed by the Crown took control of the churches, and expelled hundreds of ministers who spoke out against it. When "outed" ministers began preaching in the fields, John Nisbet and his family went to hear them.

Over time, the fire of the king's persecution of the Covenanters raged hotter. It began with the arrest and execution of the preacher James Guthrie and the Marquis of Argyll. Royal troops arrested thousands—stole property, harassed women and children, and executed hundreds. Nisbet wondered what he should do about it. "We witness our enemies overthrowing the glorious work of the Reformation," he said, "and banishing Christ out of these lands—for He alone is the head of His Church—and persecuting His gospel ministers and members."

As he prayed and pondered, Christ's words kept coming to mind: "If any man will come after me, let him deny himself, and take up his cross and follow me." John Nisbet felt duty bound to join those Covenanters who fought back. So he once again took up arms to protect the defenseless, and that is what had led him to fight at Rullion Green.

After he recovered from the injuries that he suffered in that first battle, he farmed, cared for his wife and children, and prepared to defend his family and friends. Some years later in 1678, highland clansmen who supported the king were unleashed upon the western shires where Covenanter support remained strong. They pillaged and plundered from sun up to sun down. One day four Highlanders came to Hardhill and confronted John as he worked in his barn. "Hey, Fig!" they said to him—using their derogatory term for Presbyterians who supported the National Covenant. "We've come to make you own the king." Then one of them, saw his leather boots and said, "We'll be taking those."

When they laid hands on Nisbet, he threw them off and jumped back. As the Highlanders drew their swords, John grabbed a pitchfork that he had been using to stock grain. They attacked, but Nisbet—surprising them with his strength, skill, and daring—drove them out of the barn. He knocked one to the ground, disarmed another, and chased them all off his land. He knew they would be back in force, so he took his family and fled for the hills. The next day, more than twenty armed clansmen came back. Finding the whole family gone, they stole everything of value. A few weeks later, the Highlanders left the area, and the Nisbets returned to rebuild their lives.

A year later, on a June day in 1679, a group of men, women, and children had gathered to hear a sermon not far from Nisbet's farm. They met in a field called Drumclog near Loudoun Hill. But a troop of the king's men had got word of the meeting, and fell upon them. The Covenanters had brought weapons and they rallied to resist the soldiers. One man raced off to get Nisbet. By the time John Nisbet arrived at the battle, things were going badly for the Covenanters. They had suffered many casualties and one flank had pulled back across a ditch. Nisbet saw a weakness in the enemies' line. Lifting his sword and waving his arm, he cried, "Jump the ditch and get over to the enemy!"

They rushed forward, and it turned the tide of battle. Many of the king's men fell, and the rest were forced to retreat. It was reported that Nisbet had dropped seven of the soldiers himself. "At Drumclog," one man said, "Nisbet fought boldly and briskly, seeming to cover all parts of the action."

The Covenanters rejoiced and thanked God for the victory. But the victory was short lived. Just three weeks later, the king's troops crushed the Covenanters at Bothwell Bridge. Nisbet served as a captain of a company of men and fought valiantly protecting a key position by the bridge. He killed several of the king's men and was one of the last to retreat. Nisbet suffered many wounds, but managed to escape. After the battle, soldiers scoured the countryside for him. Nisbet's bravery and effectiveness in battle led the king's council to offer a large reward for his capture. The next morning, troops over-ran Hardhill farm. Not finding John, they drove Margaret and their children from their home. Officials decreed that the Nisbet farm and all their goods were forfeit to the Crown. To magnify the cruelty, they declared that anyone who took in John Nisbet or his family or offered them so much as a cup of cold water would have their land and property seized for the king. Most of their friends and relatives wouldn't risk losing all to help them.

So the Nisbets had to wander from place to place where they were not known—sometimes living out in the wilderness and sometimes finding shelter in the cottage of a welcoming Covenanter. For four years, Nisbet's wife and four little children survived on the kindness of others. At times, Nisbet stayed with them, but never for long. He did not want the wrath of the king's soldiers to descend upon his family or their hosts. So he lived on the run—sometimes staying in the moors and mountains, sometimes resting in the cottages of Covenanters who were willing to risk it.

One man who wandered with Nisbet in the wilds described him as a quiet man who rarely talked about himself. "But he was a valiant, faithful Christian," he said, "a great examiner of the Scriptures and a great wrestler in prayer."

Nisbet found great comfort in hearing the field preaching of Cargill, Cameron, Peden, and Renwick. He said that reading the Scriptures and hearing them preached "are sweet cordials to my soul."

In December 1683, after four years of wandering—while John was still hiding in the moors—Margaret and the children found shelter in a shepherd's hut. It stood on the back of a farm owned by a sympathetic family just outside the town of Stonehouse. While there, Margaret and her daughter and three sons fell gravely ill. After a week of pain and fever, Margaret died. Her Covenanter hosts buried her at midnight in the Stonehouse churchyard, being careful to replace the dirt and sod so it would remain concealed, for government and church officials had decreed that "rebels" could not be buried in church graveyards. They were known to dig up and desecrate Covenanter bodies that had been buried in defiance of their dictates.

It was several days before the news of his wife's death and his sick children reached Nisbet. He rushed to the place. As he entered the hut, he discovered that his little daughter had passed away shortly before he arrived. He tried to speak with his sons who were sitting in the corner of the dark hut, but they were so delirious with fever that they didn't recognize him. As his friends prepared his daughter's body for burial, John leaned over, kissed her forehead and sighed, "Naked I came into this world and naked I must go out of it. The Lord is making my passage easy."

"Sir, I hope you know who has done this!" complained one mourner, remembering the cruelty of the king's men who had forced the Nisbet family from their home.

"Yes, I know well who has done it," John whispered. Then he lifted his head and said, "I know that God has done it. He makes all things work together for the good of them who love Him and keep his way."

That night, Nisbet buried his daughter next to his wife in a hidden unmarked grave in the churchyard. Then he took his sons and fled.

Later, out in the wilderness of the moors, a friend asked him if all the sacrifice and sorrow was worth it. "I am ready to live or to die for my Lord," he answered. "Although I have suffered much from prelates and false friends, yet now I would not for a thousand worlds had done otherwise."

Nisbet linked up with James Renwick, a leading Covenanter preacher and defender of the persecuted Scots. Renwick's field preaching drew hundreds to a living faith in Christ. He encouraged the people to resist the demands of the king and his bishops to control the Church of Scotland. And the king's officials hated him for it.

In November 1685, when Nisbet and some friends had gathered for prayer in a farmhouse near Fenwick, soldiers of the king attacked them. They resisted fiercely. When they were out of ammunition, they attacked, using their muskets as clubs until the stocks broke. After suffering many wounds, they were captured. As the captain gave the order to kill them on the spot, he recognized Nisbet and shouted, "Ho! —isn't this Nisbet of Hardhill? Spare his life, for the council has offered 3,000 marks for him."

They tied Nisbet's hands behind his back, and shot his friends before his eyes. "Well," the captain said to him with a sneer, "what do you think now?"

"I think as well of Christ and His cause as ever," Nisbet answered. "But I grieve and feel at a loss because I remain here while my dear brothers, whom you have murdered, are in heaven."

"You'll suffer worse!" the captain barked.

"If the Lord stands by me," Nisbet said, "and helps me to be faithful to the death, I care not what piece of suffering I might have to endure."

Guards brought Nisbet to stand trial before the king's council in Edinburgh. "We know you are acquainted with everything that the rebels do," a councilman said, "tell us all you know for the peace and good of the nation."

"I am more afraid to lie than to die," Nisbet said, "but I will not answer anything that violates my conscience."

"What do you rebels do in your meetings?" one of the judges asked him.

"We sing psalms, read the Scriptures, and pray," Nisbet answered.

"How many men and arms are at your meetings?" demanded another.

"I go to hear the gospel preached—not to take account of what men and arms are there," Nisbet said.

"Will you own the king's authority?" one of them asked.

When Nisbet explained that he would not—a councilman interrupted and said in a mocking tone, "It seems you will have no king but Mr. Renwick."

The council sentenced Nisbet to hang at the Grassmarket in Edinburgh and all his lands and property forfeited to the king. They sent him to the Tolbooth prison to await his fate. Despite being shackled in heavy leg irons that chafed his wounds, his spirit soared. "Christ wonderfully shined on me with a sense of his redeeming love, grace, and mercy," he told his friends. "The cross of Christ was always sweet and pleasant to me, but never so sweet and pleasant as now."

In his cell, John Nisbet wrote his last testimony. It was several pages long and consisted mostly of Scripture verses that explained the good news of Jesus Christ. It closed with his farewells. "I bid farewell to all my dear fellow sufferers for the testimony of Jesus who are wandering in dens and caves," he wrote. "Farewell my children, study holiness in all your ways, and praise the Lord for what he has done for me. Farewell sweet Bible, and wanderings and contendings for the truth. Welcome death. Welcome the city of my God where I shall see him, and be unable to serve him eternally with full freedom. Welcome blessed company, the angels and spirits of just men made perfect. But above all, welcome our glorious God, Father, Son, and Holy Spirit—into thy hands I commit my spirit."

An eyewitness of Nisbet's execution said, "He went rejoicing and praising the Lord."

Later, his son said that his father had lived and died by the motto: "Free, free, free grace."

28

THE TWO MARGARETS

The Solway Martyrs

Margaret MacLachlan (1622–1685)

Margaret Wilson (1667–1685)

The year 1685 is known in Scotland as "the killing times." Soldiers of King Charles II hunted down thousands of Covenanters—men, women, and children—and killed them in the cruelest ways imaginable. Their crime: they believed that Jesus Christ alone was head of the Church and sought to worship Him as the Bible directed them to.[1]

At that time, in the green hills of Galloway in southwestern Scotland, there lived a poor, grey-haired widow named Margaret MacLachlan. Her neighbors described her as a generous and devout Christian who lived humbly in a "wee cottage in the glen." Officers of the king warned her that she must forsake her Covenanter minister preaching in the fields and worship God only in the way that the king ordered. Although threatened and harassed, she would not violate her conscience. One day as she knelt worshipping the Lord, soldiers burst in and hauled her off to jail. There she endured cold and hunger until the date of her trial.

---

1. "The Two Margarets: The Solway Martyrs" is excerpted from Richard M. Hannula's *Trial and Triumph: Stories from Church History* (Moscow, ID: Canon Press, 1999).

Eighteen-year-old Margaret Wilson and her thirteen-year-old sister Agnes also refused to submit to the king's rules for worship. They avoided the king's men by living in the mountain forests and the marshes with other Covenanters. Their friends and family were ordered not to visit them nor give them food, clothes or shelter.

On a cold winter day, the two sisters, lonely, wet and hungry, sneaked into town to visit some friends. While enjoying a hot meal and warm fire, they were discovered and arrested. Margaret Wilson and her sister were thrown in prison and locked up in the "Thieves Hole," the darkest and dankest cell which was reserved for the worst criminals. With many sighs and tears, they waited two months for their trial.

On April 13, 1685 the two slight and fair teenage girls and Margaret MacLachlan stood before the court. The judge peered down at them and gave them one more opportunity for freedom. "Will you swear the oath recognizing the king as head over the church?" he asked.

"No," they answered quietly.

"Then this court finds you guilty of treason," the judge said, "for denying the king's sovereignty in the church and attending unlawful worship services and meetings in the countryside."

They stood silently.

"Kneel before the court as I pronounce the sentences upon you," ordered the judge.

When they refused to kneel, guards seized them and roughly forced them to their knees.

"Margaret MacLachlan, Margaret Wilson, and Agnes Wilson, you are guilty of treason against His Majesty's government," the judge declared, "and are hereby sentenced to death. You shall be tied to posts fixed in the sand within the tideland, and there to stand until the tidewater overflow you and drown you."

Mr. Wilson, the father of the girls, approached the bench and in a trembling voice pleaded with the judge to show mercy to his daughters. Because of Agnes's young age, the judge agreed to release her if her father paid a fine of one hundred pounds sterling. Mr. Wilson paid the large fine for Agnes; then he leapt on his horse and galloped off to Edinburgh to appeal to a higher court to overturn Margaret's death sentence.

MARGARET WILSON AND MARGARET MACLACHLAN

*"They wanted Margaret Wilson to watch the horrible death
of the old woman first."*

A small company of soldiers marched the two condemned Margarets out of prison and to a deep channel leading to the Solway, an inlet of the Irish Sea. They drove two long wooden poles deep into the sand of the tidelands, tying the older woman to the stake furthest from shore and strapping young Margaret to the pole closest to the bank. She would be able to watch Mrs. MacLachlan die. They wanted Margaret Wilson to watch the horrible death of the old woman first in hopes that she would break down and recant. Many people gathered on the banks praying that their lives might be spared.

The older Margaret said nothing as the cold seawater rose around her. She struggled to lift her head above the waves and gasped for air. One of the executioners turned to the young Margaret and sneered, "What do you think of her now?"

"I see Christ wrestling there," she answered. "Do you think that we are the sufferers? No; it is Christ in us."

Soon the waters covered the lifeless body of Margaret MacLachlan. As the rising tide swirled higher around young Margaret, she began to sing a song from Psalm 25:

> My sins and faults of youth
> Do thou, O Lord, forget:
> After thy mercy think on me,
> And for thy goodness great.
> God good and upright is:
> The way he'll sinners show;
> The meek in judgment he will guide
> And make his path to know.

Her tormentors left her hands free when they tied her to the stake and permitted her to hold a Bible. She turned to Romans chapter 8 and read aloud: "I consider that our present sufferings are not worth comparing with the glory that will be revealed in us."

Young Margaret read through to the end of the chapter: "For I am convinced that neither death nor life, neither angels nor demons, neither the present nor the future, nor any powers, neither height nor depth, nor anything else in all creation, will be able to separate us from the love of God that is in Christ Jesus our Lord."

Shortly after, the waters had risen to her neck. Soldiers waded out, loosened the ropes and lifted her up. "Pray for the King," they shouted, "for he is supreme over all persons in the Church."

"I pray for the salvation of all men," Margaret answered. "I wish no one to be condemned."

They pushed her head under the water then yanked her up again. "Pray for the King! Swear the oath," they demanded.

"Dear Margaret," called out someone in the crowd, "say, God save the King."

Her face pale and lips blue, Margaret caught her breath and prayed, "Lord, give the King repentance, forgiveness, and salvation, if it be Thy holy will."

"She has said it! She has said it!" several bystanders shouted. "Release her."

The chief officer was furious, "Let the dog go to hell! We do not want such prayers. Swear the oath," he demanded.

"No! No!" she answered. "No sinful oaths for me. I am one of Christ's children. Let me go."

"Take another drink," a soldier barked, thrusting his halberd on her shoulder and plunging her under the water for the last time. There she died for her love for Christ and her desire to follow His Word.

29

JAMES RENWICK

Last Upon the Gallows

(1662–1688)

In late July 1681, James Renwick, a young college graduate, stood in a crowd on the High Street of Edinburgh, Scotland. He came to watch the hanging of Donald Cargill, the famous Covenanter minister. Cargill's calm demeanor and clear words of faith in Christ on the gallows so moved Renwick that he decided that day to follow in his footsteps.

Renwick went to conventicles, the secret worship meetings of the Covenanters, and read the last testimonies of the Covenanter martyrs. He studied the Scriptures, prayed, and helped the persecuted church. Recognizing Renwick's gifts, the Covenanters chose him and some other promising young men to go to Holland to study for the ministry under Scottish theologians living there in exile. Soon he was ordained, and he hurried back to Scotland.

In September 1683, he began preaching on the mountains and moors, hiding from the authorities and sleeping in caves or in holes in the ground. He tramped hundreds of miles through the sleet of winter and the heat of summer to tell people about Jesus Christ. "What do you want?" he asked a gathering of folks in the western lowlands. "Salvation and deliverance? Then Christ is able to save to the uttermost all that come to Him. Lift up your eyes and come to Christ.

Now I think I hear some of you saying, 'Yes, but is He willing?' He is willing indeed! All of His promises and all of His sweet invitations tell you that He is willing and you are welcome to come. Everyone—come, he that thirst—come, he that has no money—come. It is no less than Jesus Christ who was delivered for our offenses, and was raised again for our justification, spreading forth His arms and inviting you. Come!"

His messages overflowed with love and gratitude to God. "O, what shall I say about Christ?" Renwick said. "He is the wonderful, glorious, and inestimable jewel; the incomparable pearl of great price. Let a man search through heaven and earth, he shall not find anything to compare to Christ. So then, let us be all together His and nothing of our own. If I had ten thousand times ten thousand years, I could never express all that I owe to the free grace of God. Christ is matchless!"

To those who were suffering great persecution he wrote, "We would want the path of Christ to go through a valley of roses; but it lies through a valley of tears. We would like to travel the way while sleeping; but it must be traveled while waking, watching, and fighting. But for believers, if we had to pass through ten thousand deaths and ten thousand hells, it would seem like nothing to the soul who gets a look at Christ on the other side."

Renwick spoke out against the cruel and illegal acts of the king and his officials. Because of the brutality of the king's men against innocent people, he declared that the people were within their rights to take up arms to defend themselves. Some Covenanters shunned him, saying his ideas were too rigid and divisive. Others thought he went too far in denouncing the king.

When the Privy Council in Edinburgh learned of his field preaching, they publicly proclaimed him a traitor and a rebel. The council issued a decree making it a crime to assist Renwick. Anyone who gave him supplies or food or a place to sleep or even spoke with him faced the stiffest penalties. They offered a large reward for anyone who turned him in dead or alive.

Companies of soldiers searched the countryside for him. One summer afternoon as he rode a borrowed horse with a few friends to a field meeting, a party of the king's troops surprised them. As they fled, the soldiers opened fire, wounding and capturing his friends.

But Renwick charged his horse up a hill with soldiers right behind, shooting at him. Near the crest of the hillside, he sprang off his horse and fled on foot. He scrambled on his hands and knees to a pile of stones and finding a narrow crevice in the rocks, he squeezed into it. While waiting breathless and still, he prayed and recited over and over Psalm 6:8, "Depart from me, all you workers of iniquity."

Meanwhile the king's men scoured the hill for hours, certain that Renwick was there. But after examining every nook and cranny large enough to hold a rabbit, except the small hollow where he hid, the frustrated soldiers gave up the search. They left astonished that Renwick had vanished into thin air. At nightfall, he crawled out and escaped.

In February 1685, King Charles II died and his brother James, a Roman Catholic, became king. This was in direct violation of Scottish and English law which stated that only a supporter of the Protestant Reformation could sit on the throne. James intensified the persecution begun by his brother. Renwick declared King James II a usurper, and he told his fellow Scots that they need not consider him their rightful king.

After four years of ministry on the run, Renwick was captured in Edinburgh while visiting a friend. When the captain of the guard saw his short and frail body, he said, "What! Is this the Renwick that the nation has been so troubled with?"

Guards clapped him in irons and cast him into prison. Several times, the high court brought him in for questioning. His mother came to visit him in prison and asked, "How are you doing?"

"Very well, Mother," he answered. "But since my last appearance before the court, I have scarcely been able to pray."

"O son," she said, with her brow furled and her eyes welling with tears.

"I have been so overcome with the joy of the Lord," he said with a smile, "and taken up with praising God that I've hardly had time to pray."

When Renwick first came to prison, fear of torture gripped him. But he found peace of mind through prayer. "The terror of torture has been so taken away," he told a friend, "that I would rather choose to be cast into a cauldron of boiling oil, than do anything that would go against the truth."

When he stood before the court one last time, a clerk read the charges against him. It stated that Renwick had cast off all fear of God and committed treason by denying the authority of the king and telling the people to bear arms for their defense. "Do you continue to hold to your testimony, or do you acknowledge that you were wrong?" the clerk asked.

"In the indictment," Renwick said, "it claims that I have cast off all fear of God. I deny this, for it is because I fear to offend God and violate His law that I am standing here ready to be condemned."

"Will you submit to authority?" The clerk asked. "And do you own King James to be your lawful sovereign?"

"I own all authority," Renwick said, "that has its prescription and limitations from the Word of God; but I cannot own this usurper as lawful king. His rule does not follow the Word of God and the ancient laws of the kingdom grant the crown of Scotland only to those who swear to defend the Protestant religion."

"Did you teach your followers to come armed to their meetings and, in case of opposition, to resist?" the clerk asked.

"It would have been unreasonable to do otherwise," Renwick answered. "You yourselves would have done it, if you had been in the same circumstances. I taught them to carry arms to defend themselves and resist your unjust violence."

The clerk held up Renwick's sermon notebook which soldiers took from him when he was arrested. "Do you hold to what you have written in this notebook?"

"I am ready to seal all the truth contained in it with my blood," Renwick answered.

The court found him guilty of treason and sentenced him to be hanged in the Grassmarket of Edinburgh in four days. "Would you desire a longer time?" The chief justice asked him.

"It is all the same to me," Renwick answered. "Whether the time is longer or shorter, it is welcome; my Master's timing is best."

Some friends came to his cell to urge him to compromise a little to save his life. "If you would just let a few drops of ink fall on a bit of paper," one told him, "you could be freed."

But he would not. "I rejoice," Renwick said, "that I have been counted worthy to suffer shame for the name of the Lord."

Renwick, like many other Covenanters doomed to die, wrote his final testimony and gave it to friends to encourage the church after his death. On the morning of his execution, the chief jailer told him, "Your life may still be spared, if you would simply sign this petition."

"I have never read in Scripture," Renwick replied, "where martyrs petitioned for their lives when called to suffer for the truth. In the present circumstances, I think it would be seen that I was running from the truth and rejecting Christ."

His mother and sisters came to visit him that last morning. "I see a need for my suffering at this time," he said, "and I am persuaded that my death will do more good than a long life could have done."

With a gleam in his eyes, he told them how Christ had taken away his fear of death. "The Lord has brought me within two hours of eternity," he said, "and I fear it no more than if I were called to lie down in a bed of roses."

When his mother broke down and wept, he took her hand and said, "If you love me, rejoice that I am going to my Father."

Then he offered a prayer, asking God to bless the suffering church and raise up new ministers. But mostly he praised the Lord for giving him the privilege of dying for Christ. "O, how can I contain it," he prayed, "to be within two hours of the crown of glory!"

A great crowd of spectators filled the Grassmarket to watch the execution. To keep the people from hearing him speak, guards loudly banged on drums from the time he arrived at the scaffold until he was hanged. A friend who was permitted to be with him remembered his last words.

The court assigned a clergyman to stand at his side on the gallows. "Own our king," he said, "and pray for him."

"I am soon to appear before Him who is King of kings, and Lord of lords," Renwick told him, "and He shall pour shame and confusion upon all the kings of the earth who have not ruled for Him."

Then Renwick sang Psalm 103, read Revelation Chapter 19 and prayed. "O Lord, this is the most joyful day that I have ever seen in the world!"

The loud drumming made it difficult for him to pray. "But, O Lord," Renwick said, "I shall soon be above these clouds, and then I shall enjoy You and glorify You without interruption forever. Lord, I die in the faith that You will not leave Scotland, but that You will make the blood of your witnesses the seed of your church, and return again and be glorious in our land."

As the hangman did his work, Renwick said, "Lord, into your hands I commend my spirit for You have redeemed me."

Twenty-six-year-old James Renwick was the last Covenanter to die on the gallows for his faith. His final testimony and his letters have inspired believers around the world for 300 years.

30

JOHN ELIOT

Apostle of the American Indians

(c. 1604–1690)

In October 1646, John Eliot, a Congregational minister, rode out on horseback to preach to an Indian village. The charter of the Massachusetts Bay Colony made evangelizing the Indians a primary goal and the colony's seal depicted the figure of a Native American with outstretched arms saying, "Come over and help us." Although the Massachusetts Bay Colony was sixteen years old, little had been done to preach to the Indians.

John Eliot was determined to change that. When he reached the village, he found a group of natives, men and women, boys and girls, sitting cross-legged on the floor of a large wigwam. The Indians, many of them with their faces painted with red dye and pheasant feathers in their hair, listened to Eliot preach in their native tongue. He preached for an hour, explaining to them the law of God, the punishment awaiting those who broke God's commandments and the forgiveness of sins to all who put their faith in Jesus Christ.

The Indians listened with rapt attention, for this had never happened before. It was the first time that the good news of Jesus Christ was proclaimed to them in their own language. When the sermon ended, Eliot asked, "Do you have any questions about what I have told you?"

One man asked, "How can I come to know Jesus Christ?"

"Think and meditate on what I have taught you from God's book," Eliot answered. "Think about it when you lie down on your mats in your wigwams and when you rise up and go out into the fields and woods. Pray, 'Lord, make me know Jesus Christ.' He is a God who will be found by those that seek Him with all their hearts."

"Does God understand Indian prayers?" another native asked.

"God made all things," Eliot answered. "He made all men, not only English, but Indians too. If He made them all, then He knows all that is within them, all their thoughts, words and prayers. Since He made Indians, He knows all Indian prayers."

Eliot told them that everyone is called to believe in God even though God cannot be seen. "If you saw a great wigwam would you think that raccoons or foxes built it?" Eliot asked. "Or would you think that it made itself? No, you would believe that a wise work-man made it even though you did not see him. So you should believe concerning God. When you look up to heaven and see the sun, moon, and stars—this great house that God has made—though you do not see Him with your eyes, yet you have good reason to believe with your souls that our great God made it."

After answering questions for three hours, Eliot promised to return soon. When he got home, he wrote in his journal, "A glorious and affecting sight, to see a company of perishing, forlorn outcasts, diligently attending to the blessed word of salvation."

Two weeks later, he found the large wigwam crammed with people. He began by teaching some catechism questions and answers to the Indian children. "Who made you and all the world?" Eliot asked the children. He taught them to answer "God." "Who should you look to save you and redeem you from sin and hell?" Eliot asked. The children quickly learned to answer, "Jesus Christ."

Then he preached to all the people about the character of God, the judgments of hell and the sacrifice of Christ to take away sin. The Indians sat quietly, their eyes fixed on Eliot. "Fly to Jesus Christ and repent," Eliot said, "and seek mercy and pardon for Christ's sake, and then God the Father will forgive."

The words hit their mark—many wept. After the sermon, Eliot invited them to ask questions. An old warrior with tears in his eyes said, "I am an old man and near death. Is it too late for me to repent and seek after God?"

"God has told a story in His book," Eliot replied, "about men who were hired to work in a man's field. Some began in the early morning and labored all day in the hot sun while others were hired very late in the afternoon and worked just a short time. But at the end of the day, the owner of the field paid the workers the same amount regardless of how long they had toiled in the field."

Eliot explained that God promised to forgive all who came to Him in Christ whether they came early in life or in old age. "Be assured," Eliot said, "you will find favor with God though you have lived many years in sin. Repent now, it is not too late."

He left, promising to return again in two weeks. When he arrived back at the meeting place, far fewer people came out to hear his sermon. Eliot later learned that the powahs, the Indian medicine men, had spoken out against him. "Do not listen to the teaching of these Englishmen," the powahs warned the people. "If you disobey our instructions, you will die."

The sachems, the chiefs of the people, opposed Eliot too. They feared that they would lose their prestige and authority if their tribesmen followed Christ. At one point they plotted to kill Eliot, but their fear that the English colonists would retaliate deterred them from acting on it. Instead, they harassed him and told the Indian people not to listen to him.

"I truly believe," said Eliot, "that the Lord will bring great good out of all their opposition."

Despite the threats of the sachems and powahs, some continued to hear Eliot preach. One warrior named Waban, greatly moved by the sermons, mulled the messages over and over in his mind. Soon he put his trust in Jesus Christ for the forgiveness of his sins.

Later, Waban told his people, "Before I heard of God, and before the English came into this country, I had many evil things in my heart. I never have done nor can do the commandments of the Lord, but I am ashamed of all I do. I repent of all my sins. I deserve nothing but damnation. Christ only can help me. Christ has earned pardon for me."

Eliot preached to other Indian villages too—with remarkable results. Many decided to pray to the true God alone and put their faith in Jesus Christ, no longer following the powahs. Even some of the powahs renounced their old ways and believed in Christ. "They prayed to God constantly in their families, morning and evening, with great affection," Eliot reported.

One Englishman who observed the amazing change in the Indians said, "The woods rang with their sighs and prayers."

When John Eliot arrived in the New World in 1631, he had no idea that God would use him to proclaim Christ to the natives. He had studied at the University of Cambridge where he showed a great ability for understanding Greek and Hebrew, the original languages of the Scriptures. After graduating he was ordained as a minister of the Church of England. However, at that time King Charles I tried to control the church and force unscriptural practices upon her. So Eliot, at the age of twenty-seven, left England for North America where he would enjoy greater liberty to teach, preach, and worship as he thought the Bible directed.

Soon after he landed in Massachusetts, he became the minister of the church in Roxbury, a new town a few miles south of Boston. The congregation took to him immediately. He made the theme of his preaching—the unsearchable riches of Christ. Eliot followed the practice of other Puritan ministers by frequently visiting his church members. When he entered a home, he called the children to himself and laid his hands on their heads and prayed for each one. Then he delivered to the whole family a message of encouragement from the Bible. Before leaving a home, he said, "Come, let us not have a visit without prayer. Let us pray down the blessing of heaven on your family before we go."

He began his day early each morning in prayer. He often told young people, "Be morning birds."

"He was indeed a man of prayer," a friend said of him. "He not only spent time each day in earnest prayer, but often set apart whole days for prayer and fasting. Prayer and fasting were so agreeable to him that I sometimes thought that he might inherit the name 'John the Faster.'"

A year after arriving in Massachusetts, he married Hannah Mumford. The Eliots enjoyed a loving marriage and a happy family life. They had one daughter and five sons. His son John became a preacher to the Indians. "He is a good workman in the vineyard of Christ,"

Eliot wrote about him, "my assistant in the Indian work, and a staff to my age." But John died in 1668. None of Eliot's sons survived into later adulthood.

"I have had six children," Eliot said, "and I bless God for His free grace, they are all either with Christ or in Christ."

After another of his sons died, someone asked him, "How can you bear the death of such excellent children?"

"My desire was that they should serve God on earth," Eliot replied, "but if God chooses to have them serve Him in heaven, I have nothing to object against it, His will be done."

Eliot was generous to anyone in need. After being paid his salary, he often gave a portion of it away before he got home. The church officers worried that Eliot's generosity did not leave enough money for himself and his family. One day, the church treasurer decided to put his salary into a handkerchief and tie it into as many knots as he could to prevent Eliot from giving some of it away before he reached his house. On his way, he stopped to visit a poor family, and told them he wanted to give them some money to relieve their distress. Try as he might to untie the knots, he couldn't loosen them a bit. Turning to the mother of the house, he said, "Here, my dear, take it. I believe the Lord wants you to have it all."

From the moment Eliot set foot in America the plight of native people living in spiritual darkness haunted his thoughts. He knew they needed a Savior as much as he did. "God first put into my heart a compassion for the poor souls of the Indians," he said, "and a desire to teach them to know Christ."

In 1644, he began to pour himself into the study of Algonquin, the language of the New England tribes. Eliot brought an Indian boy into his home. While Eliot taught him to read and write, the young man taught Eliot Algonquin. With the help of his Indian friend he began to master the language. "I diligently studied the difference of their grammar from ours," he said. "I would pursue a word, a noun, a verb, through all variations I could think of and thus I came at it."

After two years of study, Eliot felt ready to preach to the Indians in Algonquin. His preaching visits covered a large tract of eastern Massachusetts. Visiting the widely scattered Indian villages was difficult. He rode through swollen rivers and driving rain. "For three days I have not been dry by day or night," he wrote a friend. "At night

I pulled off my boots and wrung out my stockings. In the morning, I put them on again wet and so it continues. But God steps in and helps me."

"Visited the Indians for the past four days," Eliot wrote in his journal. "The weather was cold and snowy. I was wet for the entire time but that is a small price to pay for the privilege of taking the gospel to them. The souls of men are worth more than the whole world."

Indians who were not interested in Christianity mocked their tribesmen who followed Christ. "What do you get," they asked, "by praying to God and believing in Jesus Christ? You are as poor as we. Our corn is as good as yours, and we take more pleasure than you. If we saw that you got anything by praying to God and believing in Jesus Christ, we would do it also."

The Christian Indians asked Eliot what they should say when they were taunted in this way. "God gives us two sorts of good things," he told them. "One sort is little things and the other sort is great things. The little things are riches, such as clothes, food, houses, cattle, and pleasures. These are little things which serve our bodies for a little while in this life. But the great things are the knowledge of God the Father and Jesus Christ and eternal life and repentance and faith. These are mercies for the soul and for eternal life. Now, though God does give you the little mercies, He gives you that which is a great deal better which the wicked Indians cannot see."

The Indians planted a few crops, but relied mostly on hunting and gathering for food. Smallpox and measles killed many of them. As the Indian population shrank, the number of English immigrants increased rapidly. The Indians' suspicion and resentment of the whites grew. This made Eliot's task of preaching more difficult. But natives kept turning to Christ.

One Indian woman's strong faith and godly life impressed John Eliot. After giving birth, she became very sick. Eliot visited her several times to pray with her. "Are you holding fast to Christ?" he asked her.

"I still love God, though He has made me sick," she said. "But I have resolved to pray to Him as long as I live. I believe that God will pardon all my sins because Jesus Christ died for me. I believe that I shall go to heaven and live happy with God and Christ there."

As Eliot observed the Indians growing in faith, he said, "I could hardly refrain from tears for very joy to see the Indians' diligent attention to the Word of God."

Eliot wanted the Indians and the whites to be members of the same church and to worship together. Much to his disappointment, the colonists refused to have Indians as members in their churches, so separate Indian congregations were formed.

After a time, many of the Christian Indians wanted to leave their villages with their pagan practices and start settlements where they could live and grow in their new faith. Eliot believed, as all Englishmen did at that time, that the Indians would be better off spiritually and physically by abandoning nearly every aspect of their old way of life. So Eliot petitioned the Massachusetts Bay Colony authorities for land grants for the Indians to build their own towns. Eventually, Christian Indians with the help of Eliot and his supporters built fourteen townships. Each one included a church and school. The colonists called these townships "Praying Indian towns."

After preaching to the Indians for a few years, Eliot wrote a friend, "I do very much desire to translate some parts of the Scriptures into their language. I look at Scripture translation as a sacred and holy work, and to be regarded with much fear, care, and reverence."

Remarkably, Eliot managed to translate the whole Bible into Algonquin while pastoring his Roxbury congregation and preaching to the Indians. In 1663, the Algonquin Bible was printed in Massachusetts, the first Bible printed in any language in North America. "Prayer and pains through faith in Christ Jesus will accomplish anything," Eliot said.

John Eliot wrote a few small books describing the Indians coming to faith in Christ. The books were published in England and widely read there. People in England and the American colonies praised him and began calling him "The Apostle to the Indians." Eliot did not like the praise or the title. He referred to himself as "one of the least laborers in the Lord's vineyard."

In 1675, when Eliot was seventy years old, King Phillip's War, a clash between several of the Indian tribes and the English colonists, broke out. The fighting was fierce and many of the white settlements were wiped out. The Christian Indians sided with the colonists and helped them to fight the hostile tribes. Despite the help of the Christian Indians, many Englishmen viewed them with distrust. Fearful that the Christian Indians might join the warring tribes, the Massachusetts Council, despite the pleas of John Eliot, ordered the "Praying Indians" to Deer Island in Boston Harbor to be imprisoned for the duration of the war. The wind-swept island was totally inadequate for food, shelter, and fuel for the five hundred Indians interned there. When Eliot visited them in winter, bringing what supplies he could, he found the conditions appalling, "The island was bleak and cold," he wrote, "their wigwams poor and mean, their clothes few and thin."

For eight months, they suffered the hardships of their island prison. Finally, Eliot and some others won their release. Eliot helped them move back home. They found their settlements looted and burned, all their worldly possessions lost, and nearly every copy of the Algonquin Bible destroyed.

John Eliot never failed to support the Christian Indians. He advocated for them before the governor and the council. He spoke out when they were mistreated by the whites. Many of the English colonists resented Eliot's defense of the Indians and despised him for it.

For forty years, Eliot went out every two weeks to preach and minister to the Indians. When he reached the age of eighty-three, he found his strength declining, so he cut back his preaching trips to every two months.

When his infirmities made preaching and traveling impossible, he made himself as useful as he could in his neighborhood. Eliot took pity on the African slaves whose miserable condition burdened his heart. He arranged for the poor blacks to come to his home once a week so that he could explain to them the good news of freedom in Christ. But soon this work became too much for him.

Not long before he died at the age of eighty-five, Eliot prayed, "Lord, revive and prosper the work among the poor Indians and grant that it may live when I am dead."

His prayer was answered. A few years after Eliot's death, a New England minister reported, "In this one Massachusetts province, most of the Indians have embraced the Christian religion. There are more than 3,000 Indians in this province calling on God in Christ and hearing His glorious Word."

Thomas Shepherd, a friend and fellow minister, summed up Eliot's work well when he wrote, "God was with Eliot."